We Don't Talk about
Those Kinds of Things:

The Making of a Psychic

by

Beverly LaGorga
as told to
Ed Kelemen

Copyright 2013 Beverly LaGorga and Ed Kelemen

All rights reserved

ISBN: 1496081048
ISBN-13: 978-1496081049

All rights reserved

No part of this work may be reproduced,
stored in a retrieval system or transmitted in any
form, by any means, electronic, mechanical, photocopying,
recording, or otherwise
without the express written consent of the authors.

Published in the United States of America by
Nemeleke Publishing
New Florence, PA
2014

Dedication

This book is dedicated to my husband, John,
for all his support in what I do and for encouraging
me to write about my personal experiences.
Also to my son Jeremy for inspiring me
to help others through my book.
Thank you both for all your time
and patience in helping me.
I love you.

Acknowledgments

This book would have been impossible without the input and assistance of many people. The authors express their wholehearted gratitude to them. In particular we thank the members of the Greensburg Writers Group, a patient and gentle critique group whose guidance has made this book possible, especially members Barb Miller, Marge Burke, Mary Ann Mogus, Linda Ciletti, Judith Gallagher, and Ruth McDonald.

And an extra-special thank you goes out to Judith Gallagher of Gallagher Editorial Services for her great line edit of the manuscript. Any typos, misspellings, grammatical, or formatting errors surely have been placed here by gremlins after her edit.

The cover art is just one more example of the dynamite design work of Linda Ciletti, a graphic artist beyond compare.

We're sure there are people who have helped us that we forgot to mention. If we have left you out, it was an oversight and please accept both our appreciation and our apology.

Foreword

As a young girl I remember being asked, "What do you want to be when you grow up? Well, the last thing that would have crossed my mind was a psychic/medium. Getting here has been a long and not always enjoyable journey. I am sharing my story with you for a few reasons that are important to me.

First, this is for all of you who "see, hear, and feel" things that others don't, won't, or can't. Just because others can't have your experiences, it doesn't make you crazy, it just makes them unfortunate. Realize that you have a gift that is denied to others. Develop it and use it to help people who are in need.

Second, if you have children who tell you that they see what they call ghosts or monsters, don't discount what they are telling you. It isn't necessarily just their imagination. Maybe their vocabulary isn't developed enough to describe in adult terms exactly what they are seeing and hearing. Talk with them and remember that just because you don't understand something doesn't make it any less real.

And finally, I want everyone to know that, just because you say, "We don't talk about those kinds of things," it doesn't make them go away.

Table of Contents

Dedication	iii
Acknowledgments	iv
Foreword	v

Phase One: It Begins

Phantasms in the Bedroom	1
Precognition with the Girl Scouts	4

Phase Two: It Gets Worse

The Malicious Entity with the Cadaverous Eyes	9
Daddy's Encounter	14
Highs and Lows – Life...	15
... and Death	17
Discomfort and Joy	18
Precognition Saved My Life	19
Marriage and Luck at the Slot Machines	22
Strange Smells, Cold Spots, and Voices	25
Good-bye to the House of Terror	27
My Son Gets a Visitor from the Other Side	29
They're Baack	32
My Daddy	34

Phase Three: A Glimmering

A Psychic and "Paranormal Activity"	39
A Dream?	44
A Visit from my Dad	46
A Titanic Visit	49

Phase Four: A Breakthrough ... Maybe

My Introduction to Paranormal Investigation	53

Phase Five: Developing My Abilities

I Learn Not to Ignore My Visions	61
I Become a Paranormal Investigator	62
I Psychically Witness a Murder	66
Communing with the Other Side	67
Daddy's Visit	73
Changes	74

Phase Six: I Am a Psychic

Happenings	77
Flight 93	79
Random Knocks	81
Missing, Maybe Murdered	82
Gettysburg	89
The Soldier with the Cadaverous Eyes	90
Renewing the Search	93
Another Murder	95
Finally, an Un-Haunted House ... So Far	95
A Matriarch and a Servant, Both Long Gone	95
Some Visions Are Just Too Damn Real!	99

Phase Seven: Investigations

How Paranormal Investigations Are Conducted	*103*
One of My First Investigations	*105*
My Last Investigation with SPIRITswp	*110*
I Go to a Party that Happened 140 Years Ago	*115*
Spooked by a Snake	*123*
She Fell to Her Death	*123*
The Geyer Theater	*125*

Phase Eight: What's Next

We Talk	*133*
Glossary	*135*
About the Authors	*141*

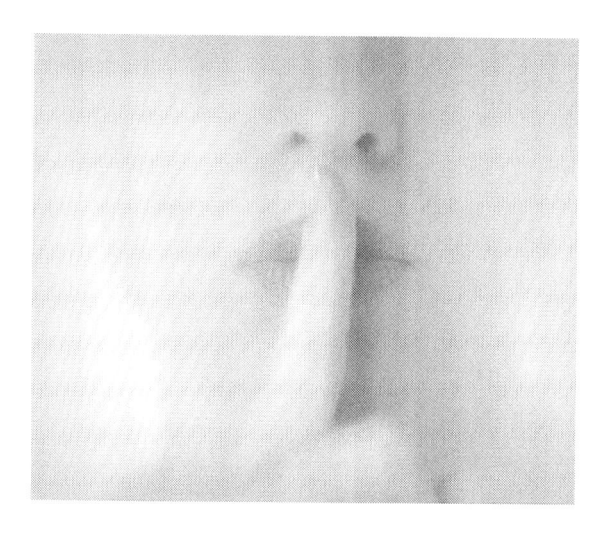

Phase One: It Begins

Phantasms in the Bedroom

It was a perfect room for two little girls. The door was at the foot of my bed and to the right. Our big old closet was along the wall to the right of my bed. Sis's bed was closest to the window, and she could look out onto the yard. You could always tell the time of year by looking at the curtains, which we changed each season. We shared a nightstand between our beds, and we each had our own dresser against the wall opposite the foot of the beds.

We even had our own television! We propped ourselves up with piles of pillows and stuffed animals. We munched on smuggled snacks and giggled at the antics of the actors on our favorite programs. Guys have their man caves, we had our girly hideaway.

Sometimes it was done Strawberry Shortcake style, sometimes Holly Hobbie, and sometimes a mish-mash

We Don't Talk About Those Kinds of Things

of both. The carpet on the floor was bubblegum pink. It was my refuge, the one spot in the whole world where nothing could bother me.

You see, *it* had started happening at night, when even the shadows of friendly things were threatening. The year was 1976 and our country was 200 years old. I was eight. Sis was five. What was *it*? Footsteps. Footsteps of someone walking about the house when nobody should have been up. I thought *it* was one of my parents, since I could see my sister in the bed next to mine sleeping blithely through the sounds.

I didn't mention it to anyone because my father routinely stayed up until after the 11 o'clock news and I hoped it was him. After that first time, nothing happened for a few nights. Then *it* happened again: footsteps. This time it was in the middle of the night, when no one had any reason to be up except to go to the bathroom. I started feeling kind of spooky then. I still didn't mention it to anyone.

As time went by and I kept hearing those footsteps in the wee hours of the morning, I began to creep out of bed to see if I could catch whoever was making these nocturnal tours. But no matter how stealthily I slid out from under the covers, as soon as my feet touched the floor, the footsteps stopped. That was scary. So I would jump right back into bed and pull the covers up over my head.

Finally, one morning I asked my parents, "Who was up in the middle of the night?"

First my mom, then my dad answered, "It wasn't me."

I *knew* it wasn't my sister. She slept through it all. But just to make sure, I asked if she had heard any strange noises like footsteps at night.

Sis answered, "Nope, I don't hear anything at night."

I thought I must be dreaming.

Then one night I woke up feeling that I was being watched.

I saw shadowy figures in the doorway of our bedroom. My refuge was violated. Our girls' hideaway was no longer safe. My mouth went dry and I ached for a drink of water, but I was too paralyzed with fear to get out of bed. It was all I could do to pull the covers up to shield my eyes.

As time went by, those feelings intensified. That eerie sense of someone watching and those dark shadowy beings standing in the doorway made for one frightened little girl. Then the shadowy things started coming right into my room! They were at the foot of my bed, beside my bed, and in the doorway of my closet.

I was trapped! My heart hammered like the drums in a marching band, my mouth was as dry as the Sahara, and I felt myself shaking apart right inside my own skin. I wasn't just frightened, I was so terrified I couldn't swallow.

My sister slept on like a satisfied breast-fed baby. I couldn't be alone with those *things,* so I awakened her. As soon as she was awake, the shadows disappeared.

This was really confusing. I heard footsteps that no one else could hear. Then I saw dark shadows that no one else could see. What was wrong with me?

I never watched spooky movies or TV shows, so I couldn't be having nightmares caused by them.

Just when I thought it couldn't get any worse, one night the skies opened up and a horrible storm crashed all around us. I was paralyzed with fright. Even with the covers pulled up over my head and my eyes squinched shut, I felt a malevolent presence standing beside my bed staring at me right through the covers. I didn't move a muscle until I was startled by the alarm clock in the morning.

At breakfast I was afraid to ask the rest of the family if they had been up and about during the night. But I had to know. And I got the answer that I dreaded. To a person, everyone said no.

We Don't Talk About Those Kinds of Things

As time went on, I noticed that the strange things happened more often and more intensely on nights when it stormed. I asked my sister if I could keep the TV on so I wouldn't feel quite as alone. That helped – a bit.

Precognition with the Girl Scouts

Those scary things weren't always there. They didn't follow me when Sis and I joined the Girl Scouts. We started as Brownies, then Juniors, Cadettes, and finally full-fledged Senior Girl Scouts. I absolutely loved being a Girl Scout! I learned so much about so many things while earning merit badges.

Kids earn merit badges by learning about a topic or an activity. Some merit badges involve volunteering, helping people, and doing community projects. Others are earned in fields like swimming, archery, crafts, camping, and life skills. I earned so many merit badges that I couldn't fit them all on my vest. Between Sis and me, we filled two vests and three jackets with badges.

Maybe because I was so busy when I was doing things with the Girl Scouts, my mind just didn't have space in it for the "other things." But they always came back.

Camping and all the things that go with it were my favorite thing. Every summer I went to Girl Scout camp and had the time of my life for a week. In 1983, ten Girl Scouts and chaperones jammed all our gear and ourselves into a van for a long summer trip all over the place. We put a sign on the van that said, "Wyoming or Bust!" and headed West.

What a trip! We camped every night at a different campground. We visited Mt. Rushmore, Crazy Horse Monument, the famous "biggest-in-the-world" Wall Drug Store, the giant arch in St. Louis, and many other places. We traveled through the Grand Tetons and the Badlands of South Dakota.

My favorite part of the trip was whitewater rafting on the Snake River. Our yelling and squealing as the waves crashed over the gunwales of the raft, soaking us, was probably heard ten miles away!

When we returned home, I even got to write an article about our trip for the monthly newsletter.

The following year, when I was sixteen, I became a camp counselor for the Girl Scouts at Laurel Mountain Camp. I camped for the entire summer, and every week was a different experience. That was because each week featured a different age group coming from a different part of the Council and having a different camping theme. What a great summer!

That winter we had a Christmas party for the camp staff that was also a kind of reunion for all of us counselors. But then "it" decided to intrude on my Girl Scout experience.

The party took place at Laurel Mountain Camp. We had all traveled some distance to get there. As the evening progressed, the weather started to turn and threaten a winter storm. Not really wanting to get stuck in the mountains, I decided to head on home. My good friend Kitty made the same decision. She lived in Greensburg, about 20 miles from me. I arrived home and went to bed.

During the night I experienced a horrible nightmare. I dreamed that Kitty had died. I awoke in a panic and cold sweat, shivering like the last leaf on a tree. The following day I learned that Kitty never made it home. She died in a car accident on an icy road in front of Seton Hill University in Greensburg, Pennsylvania.

I have been told by a psychic that Kitty is always around me to this very day, along with my grandma. I can feel their presences.

The following year I earned the highest award that the Girl Scouts can convey: the Gold Award. It's the same as a Boy Scout becoming an Eagle Scout. I achieved it with a project that I completed at the Mount Pleasant Public Free Library. My parents were fairly bursting with pride, and I was bursting with happiness.

I became an assistant troop leader, then was asked to become a troop leader. With many misgivings I had to decline. There just wouldn't be enough time for me to continue with my schooling and still be able to devote the attention to scouting that it deserves. I never lost my love of camping. Sometimes I don't know which came first, camping or Scouting. My family has had a love of the outdoors for as long as I can remember.

From Memorial Day to Labor Day, my family kept on the go, enjoying nature. One of my first memories of this was going along with my grandpap for the annual shakedown cruise of the motor home. Grandpap went over the motor home from roof to tires and bumper to bumper, cleaning and adjusting everything, making sure the tires had the right amount of air in them, topping off the oil, and checking the antifreeze.

Then he'd take it on a short trip to make sure that all systems were working properly and to fill the gas tanks. And we got to go along! Five of Us! Me, Sis, and three cousins. We all would crowd the rear window of the motor home and spend the whole little trip waving to people in cars. We just knew that they wished they were us.

Finally the big day arrived and our little convoy set out on the open road. It was usually three families traveling together. We all kept in touch on the road with CB radios. My handle was Kitten. We often stayed at a private campground in Somerset, Pennsylvania, but we took trips to Sea World, Cedar Point, Seldom Seen Mine, and many other places. And best of all, *it* never tagged along.

My favorite part of family camping was the nightly campfire. The pie irons would come out and we'd make snacks. My two favorite flavors were pizza and apple pie cooked right on the fire. How's that for opposites? Other times we made s'mores. And Sis and I showed the rest of the family how to make banana boats just like we did in the Girl Scouts.

Here's how: Take one unpeeled banana and slit it along the inside curve almost the whole length. Stuff in as many marshmallows and chocolates as you can. Wrap the whole thing in aluminum foil and plop it in the fire for a few minutes. Pick it out, open the aluminum foil, and dig in with a spoon for some pure enjoyment. My mouth is watering for one right now!

During the day we played basketball, badminton, shuffleboard, and horseshoes. And, of course, we went fishing. Daddy loved to fish, and I guess I caught the bug from him.

Daddy showed me how to put worms on a hook for bait. I even did it without squirming or saying, "Yuck." His style of fishing was to find a likely spot, set everything up, bait the hooks and put them in the water, then relax and wait for the fish.

Mom, on the other hand, was constantly moving. She liked to fish with a fly rod or to use lures, so she was in perpetual motion casting, reeling in, and casting again. Then she'd move to a new spot and do it all over again. Me, I didn't have any preference. I just liked to fish.

I remember one time when Daddy got his bobber stuck in the overflow from the lake. It got too close to the overflow screen. People are barred from entering the water near the overflow, even if they are wearing flotation devices, but that didn't stop Daddy. He wanted that bobber back. So he went back to the camper and changed into his black swim trunks. I watched the fishing poles while he changed.

When he returned, he was wearing his swim trunks and his sunglasses. He had a towel dangling around his neck and an inner tube tucked under his arm. I loved those sunglasses and had already told Daddy that I wanted them if he ever bought new ones. They were really cool-looking and had multicolored lenses that even showed your reflection.

Well, he went right in the water after that bobber, sunglasses and all. And he got the bobber back. But in the process, he flipped the inner tube over and lost our sunglasses in the murky waters. The score: one fifty-cent bobber saved, one $20 pair of sunglasses lost.

During those years, I learned to live with the strange things that happened to and around me, or maybe I just learned to ignore them. I thanked God for the Girl Scouts and for family trips, the two places in my life where I was safe from *its* intrusion.

Growing up, I couldn't talk to anyone about my experiences for fear that they would think I was crazy. You know how kids can be if they think you're different. I even wondered sometimes if I was losing my mind. That's a horrible burden for a kid. I kept asking myself, "Will it ever stop?" The answer was no.

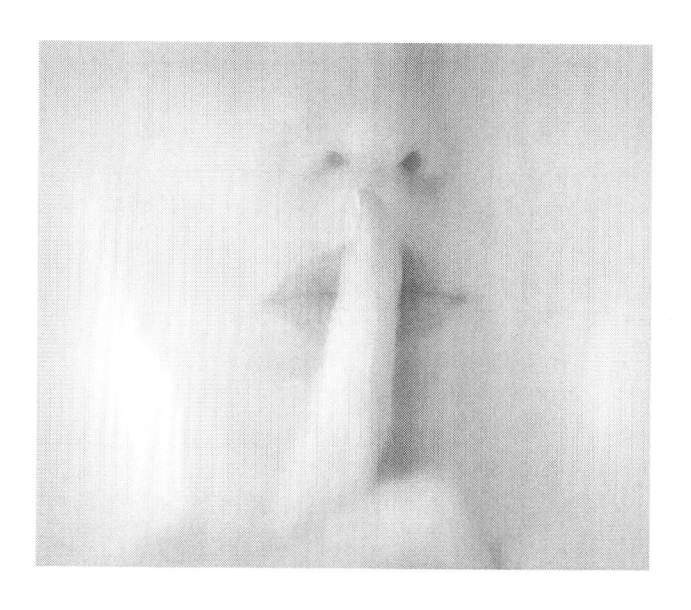

Phase Two: It Gets Worse

The Malicious Entity with Cadaverous Eyes

I started high school and began changing into a young woman, with all the intense feelings that brings. As if that weren't enough, I realized that something unusual was going on next door in my grandparents' house. Up to this point, I had been subjected to strange happenings only during the eerie hours of the night.

One sunny, beautiful day, Mom and I were on our way home from the grocery store. Walking down the sidewalk from the driveway to our front door, I stopped halfway. I had *that* feeling again. I felt that someone was watching me from my grandparents' second-story bed-room window. Even though I was afraid to, I looked up.

We Don't Talk About Those Kinds of Things

    I saw the drapes gently settle into place, as though someone or something had held them open a bit to look out. I didn't see anything else, but that feeling persisted. In the driveway we shared with my grandparents, our car was the only one there. I asked Mom if anyone was in their house.
    "No. Grandma and Grandpap went out for the afternoon," she replied.
    I told her what I had seen.
    "It's your imagination," she said.
    I left it at that. After all, I was the only one seeing and hearing things.
    A few days later I was outside cutting grass. It was my job to cut the grass in our yard and my grandparents' as well. My grandpap always watched me very closely, but Dad trusted me enough to cut our grass without supervision. I got that feeling again: I was being watched. Every so often I darted a glance at my grandparents' bedroom window. I didn't see anybody, but from that day on, I kept a close watch on that window.
    One day my mom asked me to get something from the kitchen in my grandparents' house. Even though I didn't want to, I went over there by myself. The instant I entered that house, I sensed a presence, even though the house was supposed to be empty. I got what my mother wanted and scurried back home. I told Mom that I didn't like going over there alone.
    "Why?"
    "It feels like there's somebody in the house with me, even though Grandma and Grandpap aren't home."
    She just shook her head and went back to whatever she was doing.
    A few days later, she asked me to get something else over there. I went and got it. Then she sent me over for something else. Then something else. I was reluctant, but I

went again and again. It got to the point that I knew exactly where that presence was as soon as I walked through the door. It was a male presence, and he knew exactly where I was too. If he wasn't waiting for me in the doorway between the living room and the kitchen when I walked in, he would soon begin laughing. I located him by tracking the origin of that laugh.

It wasn't an ordinary, happy laugh. It was a deep-throated, snickering, insidious, malevolent laugh. I can hear it now. The first time I heard it, I was so scared that I ran out of the house, not even knowing or caring if I closed the door after me.

As I made more trips to my grandparents' house when they weren't there, his evil laugh got worse. It got deeper and louder. I not only heard it, I felt it as well.

Then came the threat. While I was standing in the kitchen, the knife drawer opened. One of the knives flew all the way across the room and slammed into a cupboard door. I blinked my eyes and everything was back the way it had been. But I was determined never to go over there alone again.

I asked my mother about the strange things that happened in that house.

"We don't talk about those kinds of things," was her reply.

"Why?" I insisted.

"I grew up in that house. If there was anything going on, I would know it."

It wasn't really an answer, and we both knew it, but the subject was closed. I wasn't at all sure I believed her, but I was sure she wasn't going to tell me anything more.

Since I refused to go over to my grandparents' house alone, my mother said for me to take my sister. That didn't work out so well because Sis always had some excuse.

We Don't Talk About Those Kinds of Things

Mom was usually in the middle of cooking or baking something when she asked me to go. You see, if the mood to bake or cook something struck her, she just jumped right in doing it without checking to see if she had all the ingredients. Most of the time she would come up short on something, but she never worried about it because my grandmother would have it next door.

For a while Mom was on a sewing kick. Taking advantage of this, my grandma had asked her to hem a pair of pants for her. So Mom asked me to get those pants from the upstairs of my grandparents' house.

"Not by myself," I said.

"Ask your sister to go with you."

I did, but she wouldn't go. I told Mom that I was going to ask Daddy, but she said not to. I thought that was strange, but I didn't question it at the time. I screwed up my courage and went on over myself.

I stayed outside the door for a few moments to take a few deep breaths and try to stop shaking. After settling my nerves a bit, I opened the door and went in. "Leave me alone," I called out. "I'm just going to be here for a minute to get one thing, and then I'm out of here."

I hoped the male presence would hear me. I ran upstairs and got the pants my mom wanted as fast as I could. Then I turned around and ran back down the stairs with my heart exploding in my chest. I didn't even go to the door I usually used. Instead I went to the closest door, the heavy old wooden one at the bottom of the steps. I unlocked it and pulled with all my might. It wouldn't budge. That loud, insistent laughter from the male entity was right behind me.

I pulled so hard on that door that I thought I'd fall over backwards when it finally opened. I knew the door was unlocked, but still it wouldn't give way. He was locking me in just to show me he could. An eternity passed before that door finally opened, even though it was probably only a few minutes.

As soon as the door reluctantly creaked open on its hinges, I escaped as quickly as my feet would carry me.

Breathlessly, I told my mother that I'd left by the back door and didn't remember closing it. She wasn't happy, but I didn't care. I had gotten out of there.

But my own house was still no refuge. I couldn't even get any respite in sleep. I was tormented by nightmares that got worse as time went by.

Then my grandma became ill with cancer. I often went over to sit and talk with her. For a long time, there was no trouble as long as she was there with me. But one day we were sitting on the couch talking when *it* happened again. I felt that male presence standing in the doorway between the living room and hall. I looked where I knew he was standing. I saw nothing, but I got really cold.

As I continued to talk with Gram, I felt something on my other side. The seat on the couch was indented as though someone were sitting there. Instinctively I moved closer to my grandma and asked her about the strange things that happened in her house.

"We don't talk about those kinds of things," she told me.

I tried, I really did, to get some information from her. I even started telling her about some of the things I'd seen and heard.

She did not want to hear it. "We don't talk about those kinds of things" was the only answer I got. So I let the subject drop.

We Don't Talk About Those Kinds of Things

Daddy's Encounter

When I got home, I asked Mom why I couldn't ask Daddy to go over to Grandma's with me. After some wheedling, whining, and cajoling, she finally told me.

When Mom and Dad were first married, they were visiting Mom's parents. On the very first night they stayed there, Dad saw a soldier standing at the foot of their bed looking at them.

That was the last night Dad ever spent in that house. He refused to talk about what he had seen to anyone, even Mom, and he said that he would never go into that house unless he had to, and never, ever alone. Until the day he died, he never did.

What a relief! Finally there was someone besides me who had experienced strange things in that house. I wasn't crazy! Though a great load had been lifted from me, I was still confused. What exactly did my dad see and hear? What kind of soldier did he see? I will never know the answers to these and many more questions because I was told not to ask him.

The nightmares continued.

As time passed, I was able to glean more information about the male entity in that house. I started to piece together what I was seeing in my nightmares. I would remember his empty black eyes staring at me and his unnerving laugh. He was a Confederate soldier. Eventually I was able to visualize his presence clearly. He was a hefty, redheaded man with a scruffy beard. He wore a gray Confederate uniform. His long coat had golden buttons and a general's emblem on the collar. He wore white gloves and carried a gold sword with tassels hanging from it. Gray pants with a yellow stripe were tucked into his shiny black boots. A dirty white hat was pinned up on one side. The front of the hat had a pin with crossed swords on it.

14

I later found out that I was describing a general of a Confederate cavalry unit. I'll never forget the horror and fear that coursed through my body as he pinned me with those lifeless black eyes.

Highs--and Lows
Life ...

When I graduated from high school, I went away to Sawyer Business School in Pittsburgh. For a while, things seemed to get normal for me. I was so busy with school and studying that there just didn't seem to be room in my mind for much of anything else. The only threat I remember from that time was a feeling that something bad was going to happen. I chalked it up to woman's intuition.

But when I went home on weekends, the watcher in the window of my grandparents' house continued to menace me. Somehow the menacing entity that lurked in and around the two houses gathered strength from thunderstorms and multiplied those evil emanations that frightened me so.

June 1987 was one of the best months of my life. For eight months, I had made the long weekly commute to Pittsburgh, nearly 40 miles away, attending business school. I graduated that month and landed a job at a local motel complex doing what I was trained to do. I started work the very day after my graduation. I was elated, but that wasn't even the best part.

The best part was that, when I started that job, I met my husband, John. He was the night auditor and I met him on my very first day at work. I got to work early and there he was, waiting to be relieved so he could go home. The first time I laid eyes on him, the question crossed my mind, "Who is that hunk who is a double for Erik Estrada?" (In case you're too young to know, Erik Estrada was the star of the popular TV show *CHIPs*. He was also the heartthrob of every teenage girl in the country.)

As luck would have it, I was training on the morning shift, and part of my job was to relieve the night shift auditor. As I said, John was the night-shift auditor. I made it my business to be early for work just so we could talk. And he stayed a little late.

Soon after finishing my training for the daytime position, I learned that the other night auditor was retiring. Management at the motel offered me the job, with John as my trainer. You know I took that job. Auditing wasn't the only thing I studied during training!

After a couple of weeks, John invited me to a Fourth of July party that he and his brother were hosting at the log cabin they lived in a few miles away in Bear Rocks. I'm not much for parties, but there was no way I was going to miss a chance to spend time with John. So of course I went to the party, and we started dating.

Usually we went out for dinner and a movie. I still remember the first movie we went to see together, *Fatal Attraction*. Maybe not the best choice for date night.

Often, when the weather was agreeable, we went for nice long rides in John's pride and joy, his 1976 Silver T-roof Corvette, a five-speed with a black leather interior. I loved it when he would open it up on Three Mile Hill. It was like blasting off in a rocket ship. He loved that car so much that he never even took it out of the garage unless the sun was shining.

We worked together and dated for a few months. Then I got an interview for my dream job with a major airline. I aced the interview, got the job, and was scheduled to start in a new city the following January. I was so excited that I nearly jumped clear out of my skin! Although he was supportive, John didn't exactly share my enthusiasm.

... and Death

Have you ever noticed how every high in life seems to have a corresponding low, just to keep things in balance? This time, the low was the absolute lowest. Grandma passed away in August of 1987. This was a hard time for me, but I never told anyone how bad it really was. She was the first person I loved who died. My grandma was a second mother to me. I could talk with her about anything in the whole world (except what happened in her house).

The sudden loss of my friend and confidante left me feeling lost, helpless, and confused. Death had never visited me in such a way before. The whole family was affected. She was our matriarch, our source of strength, our font of wisdom, and the object of our unconditional love. Grandma treated everyone in the community with kindness, and she was respected by one and all. Sometimes I would marvel at how much power was concentrated in her little body.

I remember her clear, wonderful voice as we sat together singing gospel songs. I remember how her face would brighten with happiness when I would bring her, still warm from the oven apple turnovers that I'd made for her. To this day, the sound of gospel music and the aroma of apple turnovers bring back those days and I miss her all over again, as though I lost her just yesterday.

So it was hard for me. I especially didn't like being in the funeral home. It wasn't until the last day of visitation that I was able to force myself to look at Grandma's body.

I felt myself being watched—by whom or what I didn't know. Every time I looked in the direction where I thought the watcher was located, I saw nobody. I felt very uncomfortable. Funeral homes are not the most comfortable places under the best of conditions, and this sense of being under constant observation by an unseen being only made it worse.

Discomfort and Joy

While time doesn't necessarily heal all wounds, it does numb them. So the months flew by and I moved 450 miles away from home to Hartford, Connecticut, in January. John and I maintained a long-distance relationship. It was hard, but we made it work.

I really wasn't comfortable being alone and living so far from home. My new roommate spent a lot of time visiting friends in our apartment building. It didn't bother me when she spent time with our friends who lived down the hall, but I always got a really bad feeling in the pool area. I felt someone watching, watching, watching me. The old feeling of terror settled on me once again.

I was afraid to tell my family or my future husband about those feelings because I feared that they would make me come right back home. I loved my job and didn't want to leave it. I did tell my friends and roommate that I felt as though we were being watched or followed. From that day onward we never went anywhere alone, even if we had to call our friends down the hall to go with us.

Eventually my roomie went away on a week-long trip. I was completely by myself, just me and my sense of impending doom. That week seemed to last a month. I tried my best to stay locked up in that apartment the whole week. I called John a zillion times just to get comfort from hearing his voice.

Soon after my roommate returned, I made a trip home. It was such a relief to be away from the apartment building. John and I were watching a beautiful sunset at a lake when he surprised me with a proposal. Of course I accepted. We were engaged to be married! I was so happy that I forgot all about my fears.

But like all things, good and bad, my vacation came to an end. As soon as I arrived back at the apartment building, that feeling of dread and doom returned. I'd been there almost a year and I was trying to get a transfer home. The only opening was in Dallas, Texas, but I wasn't about to move that far away!

I was trying to finagle a way to get home for Christmas. Something dreadful was approaching like an out-of-control truck coming down a mountainside. I knew something very bad was about to happen to me; I just didn't know what.

I packed as many of my belongings as I could into my car and drove home. As soon as the holidays were over and I went back to the apartment, I gave my two weeks' notice at work. I was petrified for the entire two weeks.

I moved back home at the beginning of 1989 and started planning our wedding. The danger I knew about at my grandparents' house seemed a relief compared to the unknown dread that permeated my apartment.

Precognition Saved my Life

At about this time I started to have premonitions. They were like disconnected scenes from a movie, or unbidden thoughts that took over my consciousness. For example, one time when I was cooking dinner, I started thinking about Nadine, an old friend I hadn't talked with in ages. I wondered what she was up to. Soon the phone rang. It was Nadine!

"Hi, Bev. I was just thinking about you and decided

to give you a call. How are things going?"

    This got to be such a regular occurrence that, when someone popped into my consciousness without prodding, I knew they would be calling soon. I still didn't understand what was happening to me or why. Since none of it made any sense to me, how could I explain it to anyone else without sounding crazy?

    I kept thinking of my mother's and grandmother's mantra: "We don't talk about those kinds of things."

    Overall it was a happy time for me, what with making plans for the wedding and all. John and his brother were living in a cozy log cabin in the middle of the woods at the end of a dead-end road with only one neighbor, catty-corner across from them. After our wedding, it was to be our house.

    One day a few months before our wedding, John was at work and his brother was staying overnight at their parents' house. I went to the cabin to surprise John with a love note that he would find when he arrived home from work at eleven that night. I wished that I could be there in person to tell him how much I loved him, but I had to be up early, really early, for work the next morning. So a note would have to do.

    While writing the note, I got an uneasy feeling. The trees that surrounded the cabin no longer felt cozy. They now felt foreboding, as though they were hiding some indefinable evil. And that uneasy feeling intensified. Before I finished my chatty note about how my day had gone, I could feel unseen eyes boring into me.

    Something was watching me with malevolence in its heart. It was outside looking in through the sliding glass doors in the living room. Fearing for my safety, I made sure that the security bar was in place in the track of the sliding doors and that the other door was locked.

    The feeling kept getting worse. I had to get out of

there. Impending danger washed over me like surf at the seashore. I sensed multiple entities out there in the woods that seemed to be closing in around the cabin. After double-checking that the doors were locked, I hightailed it out of there and went home. I even forgot to leave John the note.

My phone rang at 11:45 that night.

"Bev, it's John." He didn't sound like his usual self.

"What's the matter, hon?"

"Were you over at the cabin today?"

"Why?"

"We got robbed."

Oh, my God was all that ran through my mind as I threw on some clothes and rushed to be by his side. I didn't know what I could do, but I wanted to support him in any way possible.

The whole place had been turned upside down. When the police arrived to investigate and take our statements, they told us that because so much had been taken in the short time between my departure and John's arrival, more than one person had to be involved. I was shocked.

I was afraid to spend the night alone at that cabin ever again. Instead of making fun of me for being scared, John gave me a beautiful chow-chow puppy named Prince for Valentine's Day. He and his brother trained Prince, and I absolutely loved that cuddly fluff ball of companionship and protection.

Woe betide anyone who would threaten either me or my home.

Marriage and Luck at the Slot Machines

Time flew, and before I knew it, May 1990 arrived. I thought I would burst with happiness!

The night before my wedding I had a dream, and not the kind you would expect a bride-to-be to have. I dreamed that my husband got into a fistfight at our wedding reception.

In reality a few sticky and funny things happened on the wedding day, but everything turned out beautifully, and there was no violence.

In the reception line after the wedding, Grandpap, with tears in his eyes, said, "I wish your grandma was here to see you get married."

I hugged him as tight as I could and told him, "Grandpap, Grandma *is* here with us. She did see us get married."

I didn't tell him that Grandma was standing behind my right shoulder. I don't know how I knew she was there. I didn't see her, I just felt her.

John's parents agreed to stay at the cabin and take care of Prince while we were away, so it was off to Las Vegas and the Grand Canyon for our honeymoon. Bright and early Las Vegas time, the phone in our hotel room woke us with its insistent ringing.

Bleary-eyed and still sleepy from the excitement of our wedding, the reception, and the plane ride, John answered the phone. It was my new father-in-law. He wanted us to know that Prince had pushed him out of bed at 7:00 a.m. to go outside and wouldn't take no for an answer.

"Well that's when he usually goes out. He's a creature of habit. I told you that before we left," John said to his father.

After he hung up, John and I got a great chuckle out of the phone call.

We spent the rest of the day exploring Las Vegas and had a so-called light lunch back at the hotel. John got a sandwich and I got a chef's salad that would take a football team two days to consume. Some light lunch! That night we went to a dinner show featuring the Oak Ridge Boys, one of our favorite groups.

The next morning we had a buffet breakfast at our hotel, then put on our gambling shoes and started walking. Our first target was the Imperial Palace. After we broke the bank there, John said, we would hit the other casinos in town.

He was joking. I knew absolutely nothing about gambling, casinos, table games, or slot machines so John decided to show me how to play slot-machine poker. We started at a dime machine and played a few games until he thought I had gotten the hang of it, though I really hadn't. Then he moved me up to a quarter machine.

After watching me play for a bit, he headed for the blackjack table, leaving me to my own devices.

"I'll be right over there," he said, pointing at one of the tables. "That way I can keep an eye on you, and you'll be able to see me as well."

I embarked on my gambling career with a pile of quarters and started playing. I won some, lost some, and enjoyed myself keeping pretty much even.

Then I noticed something on the machine called a double-up button. I got a pair and knew that I had already won something, so I decided to hit the button to see what would happen. The dang thing doubled my winnings!

Hey, this was fun! I didn't even stop to think why there would be a button designed to double your winnings, I just used the ole thing. I was having so much fun that I forgot to keep an eye out for John.

We Don't Talk About Those Kinds of Things

After a while, a bunch of people gathered around to watch me play. One of them was a casino security guard. I was so intent on the game that I didn't even notice them.

John saw the crowd from where he was playing blackjack. He cashed in and came over to ask the security guard if I had done something wrong.

"Heck, no," she said. "Do you know her?"

"That's my wife," John replied.

"Look how she's playing. She's doubling up on big winners."

John and the security guard watched me play another hand doubling up.

"She really doesn't know what she's doing, does she?" the security guard asked John.

Just as he replied, "No," the slot machine lost its mind. It started flashing a crazy light, making some kind of weird loud noise, and shooting coins out like an avalanche of silver. I thought I'd broken the slot machine.

I told John that all I wanted to do was to stop all the noise, gather up whatever I had won, and get out of there. Someone handed me an empty cup and I filled it, along with the cup I had originally brought with coins. When I turned to leave, I noticed all the people standing around watching me.

"John, why are all these people here? And what's that security guard doing here? Am I in some kind of trouble?"

"Nope," John said, "You aren't in any trouble. People always come over to watch a big winner play, and the security guard is here to escort you to the cash window with your winnings."

"Really?" I said. "How much did I win, anyway?"

It hadn't sunk in yet that I'd made money while having fun. It didn't sink in completely until we were back in our room. While having a bit of fun at a slot machine, I had paid for our entire honeymoon and then some.

Years later I still get asked whether my psychic ability helped me win that day. "Nope," I say. "I think it was just blind, dumb luck." Actually, my ability may have had something to do with it. I just don't know.

When we returned from our honeymoon, my mother told me that the guy who managed our reception hall had run off with all of the facility's funds. That was when I learned that my husband had had a big blow-out with him right before the wedding. My dream had come true—albeit without bruised knuckles, and a day early.

Strange Smells, Cold Spots, and Voices

After only six months of marriage, my health started to go downhill a bit. Luckily, nothing weird was happening to distract or frighten me. But each month brought yet another health issue.

In early 1993, Mom told me that Grandpap was having a terrible time dealing with Grandma's passing. He barely knew what to do without her. Grandpap was a tall, physically imposing man with an iron will and a stubborn streak a mile wide. It broke my heart to see him so sad missing grandma.

At the time, I was training to be a Certified Nurse's Aide. I wanted to help Mom take care of Grandpap, but in order to do so, I had to enter that dreaded house, the source of so many of my childhood fears. The house of malevolent visions, snickering laughs, footsteps, and danger. But Grandpap needed my help, so I steeled myself and did what had to be done. At least I wasn't the only real, live person there.

I spent a lot of time there, making sure he had enough to eat and doing some housekeeping. To my relief, I didn't experience anything suspicious. I guess I was so preoccupied with my health and my grandpap's health that I just didn't have any energy left over for spiritual contacts.

The midpoint of the year found me working at a nursing home. One day I was walking along the hallway, checking on the residents in their rooms and making sure that everything was okay. Someone passed me walking the opposite direction. I didn't recognize her, so I turned around to introduce myself to this new resident and welcome her– only to watch her dissolve into thin air.

I was so shocked that I couldn't even move for a minute or two. When I regained my composure, I looked around to see if anyone else had seen her. Of course there was no one around.

Later that month, I was doing room checks in that unit again. One of the rooms I walked into was extremely hot, the kind of heat that comes from a fireplace in a small room, hotter than any space heater would make it. I also smelled smoke. This was a nonsmoking facility, and it wasn't tobacco smoke that I smelled anyway. Even though it was enough to make my sensitive nose and throat burn, there was no smoke to be seen.

I asked around and was told by a long-time employee that that room had been nearly destroyed by fire several years earlier. I was flabbergasted!

I don't know what it was with that unit, but a few weeks later I found myself walking through freezing cold spots. There were also footsteps, which would get closer and closer. Just when they seemed about to walk over me, the sound would stop and a cold breeze would wash over me.

From time to time I'd hear my name when nobody was around to call it.

In a joking manner, as though they didn't bother me, I mentioned these occurrences to a co-worker. "Oh, yeah," she replied, "things like that always happen around here. Especially on the lower level."

Hallelujah! It wasn't just me! I wasn't losing my mind.

By early 1993, Grandpap could no longer stay in his own home. He was admitted to the very nursing home where I worked. In less than a month, he died there. If anyone ever died from a broken heart, it was Grandpap. Finally he and Grandma were happy together again.

Good-bye to the House of Terror

That old house that had caused me so much terror was put up for sale. It was on the market for a year before a young couple bought it. After giving them a month to settle in, I talked with the new owners. They were in love with the place. They planned on renovating it back to its 1800s-style roots. In a roundabout way I asked if they had noticed anything strange. "Nope," they said. "Everything is great."

A few months later, I found out that John had tried to buy that house for me as a surprise. When he told me, it was such a shock to my system that my heart skipped a beat and I gasped for air. For a moment I actually forgot that it had already been sold. John apologized for being unable to swing a deal on the house. I didn't even realize I was holding my breath until I gave a great sigh of relief.

"Why do you sound relieved at the bad news?" John asked.

I said that I had had terrifying experiences in that house.

John asked, "How were you going to be able to live there if the deal had gone through?"

"I couldn't," I replied.

He never mentioned it again, but I gave thanks that

the deal had failed to materialize. John didn't question me any further. I'm glad that I didn't have to explain why to him. I wasn't sure what to tell him. Should I explain to him exactly what had happened and have him not believe me? John wouldn't understand what I went through, I thought. Nobody really understands, so why bother? It just goes back to "we don't talk about those kinds of things."

Early on in our marriage, John and I lived in a rented duplex. One morning he came home from working the night shift and went to bed. He was now a night auditor for a different hotel. I was downstairs in the kitchen when I heard my name being called.

"Bev?"

I went to the foot of the steps and hollered, "What do you want?"

There was no answer, so I hollered again. Still no answer. So I went up to the bedroom, only to find John asleep. I woke him up and asked, "Have you been calling me? What do you want?"

"I didn't call you. I'm trying to sleep," he replied groggily.

I figured that he must've called out in his sleep, so I just apologized for waking him. He went back to sleep, and I went back downstairs.

I looked outside, but there was no one around. It was early in the morning and I hadn't even turned on the TV yet, so it wasn't coming from there. It was a man's voice, clear as a bell. Who had called out my name? Out of all the people in the world, I thought of my grandpap. But I couldn't ask him what he wanted unless I could talk to ghosts.

My Son Gets a Visitor from The Other Side

The smoke at the nursing home was just the first assault on my sense of smell. Then I began smelling things at home. Neither my husband nor I smoke. I am very allergic to tobacco smoke, so there is none of it in my house.

Nonetheless, from time to time I would smell the distinctive, nauseating odor of cigarettes and cigars. Sometimes while sitting on the couch to relax or watch TV, I would suddenly smell flowers or perfumes. I'm allergic to flowers and strong perfumes too, so we don't have any real flowers in our home, just the artificial kind.

I've been told that a person's sense of smell can trigger the strongest memories, but it just made me want to choke and sneeze.

One night John and I were relaxing together on the couch, winding down from the day, watching TV. Suddenly we saw a ball of bright white light move across the top of the wall opposite us. That wall has the only window in the room, so it wasn't light coming in through it. Then we thought it might be the reflected light from a car's headlights coming through the window. But there was nothing in the room reflective enough to produce that effect. There was no logical explanation, so we just shrugged it off and never spoke of it afterward. John did say that, if I told anyone what we saw, he would deny that it ever happened. I guess you could say he's a skeptic.

We got pregnant with our son, and that starter house was just too small for raising a family. We found a nice home for rent in Jeannette and moved right in. Jeremy was born. I hadn't been bothered by strangeness for a while, and I came to believe all my weird experiences were in my past. Our son grew from an infant to a not-quite-toddler.

We Don't Talk About Those Kinds of Things

We had our little family, and we were happy.

I'd hear Jeremy laughing and giggling in his crib, so I'd go in and play with him. He always had his hands reaching up in the air as though he wanted to be picked up. So I would pick him up and we would twirl around and play and laugh for a while. It was a really happy time in my life.

When he learned to stand in the crib, he would stand in a corner and reach his hands up, giggling and making nonsense sounds all the while. It was as though he was talking to someone I couldn't see. I tried to ignore it, though I did feel a twinge of uneasiness.

On Jeremy's third birthday he got a battery-operated toy workbench that talked. He loved that toy! He played with it constantly. The batteries quickly ran out of juice. Well, that darn thing woke me up from a sound sleep with its talking in the middle of the night. I got up and switched it off to get a little peace. Later, when I was more awake, I thanked John for changing the batteries. He didn't reply; he must not have heard me.

The next morning Jeremy was playing with his workbench again. He started fussing a bit when it wouldn't talk to him, so I flipped its switch, gave it back to him, and went into the next room to fold clothes. I can't remember whether or not it started talking. I turned it off later to give it a rest and went on about my day. It was sure talking again that night. It woke me from a sound sleep again. This time I took out the batteries and went back to bed. I didn't care how it was getting turned on in the middle of the night, I just didn't want it waking our son.

We were out shopping, doing chores, visiting all day, so the workbench didn't get played with.

I just made sure that my son's favorite toy was in the crib with him that night so he'd go to sleep without any problems. Come those dark hours between midnight and dawn, the thing woke me again with its babbling, for the third night in a row. This was getting old! I put it downstairs, out of hearing range, and went back to bed.

Before leaving for work in the morning, I asked my husband to check the workbench and see what was the matter with it. I told him that it had waked me up three nights in a row. When I got home that evening, John told me the workbench didn't even have batteries in it. So how could it wake me during the night? He said I must have been dreaming.

Dreaming or not, it hadn't found its way downstairs on its own. I knew I didn't walk in my sleep. And I was sure it hadn't taken out its own batteries. I gave the workbench a special place on a shelf in the farthest corner of the cellar.

One day Jeremy and I were looking through family photos. When we came to a picture of my grandfather, he pointed at it and said, "Grandpap."

"What?" I said, dumbfounded.

"Grandpap," he repeated, pointing again at my grandpap, his great-grandpap, who died years before he was even born.

I was unnerved. My son told me he and Grandpap played with his workbench in his room all the time. I didn't know what to do, so I threw the workbench out in the garbage.

I realize now that reaction doesn't make sense, but I didn't know what else to do. What would you do if your child said that he or she played with a toy with someone who had died before they were born? It made me a little frightened to think that I was the only one hearing it going off and there were no batteries in it. Not to mention that he was playing with a spirit. How do you explain that one? I was at a loss for words. I thought the best thing that I could do was not have it anymore. That should solve the problem.

They're Baack

Remember those footsteps I used to hear as a little girl? They came back. I could hear someone walking around downstairs in the wee hours. Then I heard feet coming up the stairs to the second floor. At first I thought someone had broken into our house. That old feeling of having my refuge violated was back, but now I had a child and a husband to worry about too.

I awakened John and told him I thought we had a burglar in the house. I got out of bed and ensured Jeremy's safety while my husband checked the downstairs. He came back up and told me, "I checked all the doors and windows. Everything is fine. There is no burglar."

He then lay down, rolled over, and slept the sleep of the just. I tossed and turned until oblivion overtook me.

This scenario happened several times, so many in fact that I stopped waking John. I wondered whether they were the same entities who used to wake me when I was little or whether this house had its own troop of spirits.

One night we got our son settled early and prepared for a nice quiet evening in front of the TV. We didn't really care what was on. We just wanted some alone time together on the couch. It was nice and cozy. All the curtains were closed, and one small light was on in the living room.

We were completely relaxed when – wouldn't you just know it – another white light appeared. This time, instead of a ball of light, it was a streak of light that ran across the top of two adjacent walls, then disappeared. I looked at John; he looked at me. We tried to figure out what it might have been but couldn't come up with a satisfactory explanation, so we went back to watching TV. But it weighed on me, another straw for the camel's back.

Another year passed. I still heard footsteps and occasionally someone calling my name. I felt as though someone or something was following me about the house. I would stop abruptly, then spin around to catch it. For a short while I thought it was my son playing games with me, but when it happened, he was always in a different part of the house playing or helping his dad.

Paranoia settled on my shoulders like a heavy cloak. There was so much of this unexplainable stuff going on in my life. I decided I'd have to try harder to ignore it. It was déjà vu all over again. My childhood was haunting me. I was being overwhelmed by all the strangeness: The footsteps. The shadows. My name being called out. The premonitions. I couldn't tell anyone, even John, or they'd know that I was crazy.

Then I remembered that I wasn't alone the times the light ran across the room. My son was saying he talked with my grandpap, who passed long before he was born. My mother told me never to ask my dad to go into my grandparents' house. And both Mom and Grandma had admonished me, "We don't talk about those kinds of things."

They weren't oblivious to those things; they were purposely avoiding them. Something real had to be going on. I just didn't know what or why. I wondered if there was anybody out there who could help me.

As the new millennium approached, my premonitions became more frequent and more intense. Most of the time I couldn't make sense of what was bombarding my psyche. I was getting only bits and pieces, like one frame from a movie flashing across my consciousness at a time. It was excruciating to try to concentrate enough to get a bit more information. Every so often I would get that additional information, but usually I just got a migraine.

Then came the day I got a premonition that was clear as a bell. To this day, I wish it had never arrived.

My Daddy

On November 26, 2000, at 5:10 pm., I received a phone call from my mom. I could tell immediately that something was horribly wrong. In a torrent of emotion, Mom gave me the absolute worst news I could fathom. I was barely able to understand what she was saying.

It was Dad's sixty-fifth birthday, and his present from his doctor was a diagnosis of lung cancer. As soon as it sank in, I knew that Dad was going to die. No matter what Mom said about his chances, chemotherapy or whatever, I knew it was over. My dad was going to die. I am well aware that many people survive cancer these days, and the doctors were holding out hope. But I *knew* Death was coming for my dad.

I could no longer even hear the words my mother was saying. All I could think of was that this would be our last holidays, and Jeremy's last birthday with Dad.

Then I remembered I was still at work. I still had an hour to go on my shift. I went through the motions like an automaton. Shock protected me until I finished work that evening.

Once I left work, it hit me: this is Daddy's last birthday. The tears started flowing and I didn't even try to stop them. Next summer would be the last camping trip for Dad to teach Jeremy how to fish. A sliver of a smile escaped through my tears when I thought of how Jeremy idolized his Pap-pap, even though he was only three years old. They were closer than chocolate coating on an ice cream bar.

That damn premonition reared its head, and I knew

there would be no more camping trips. Daddy wouldn't be able to teach Jeremy to fish. Daddy wouldn't even be here for Memorial Day.

Then I made a mistake. I asked myself just how long Daddy had to live. The month of May burned itself into my consciousness. To this day I wish I could take it back. I couldn't share this with anyone. It would devastate my family – if they even believed me. Most likely they wouldn't believe. I might even be accused of giving up on Dad. I had to live with this information weighing on me, with no one to share the burden.

I eventually told John that I'd had a horrible dream that my dad was not going to live. John told me that it was just that. A horrible dream. But I knew it was a premonition. Down in my heart I knew.

I was so close to my dad that I couldn't live with what I knew. But I had to. Imagine what it was like for me to watch him go through the pain of months of therapies and chemo treatments, knowing, *knowing* that it was all to no avail.

Through those all-too-short months, I maintained my sanity by reminiscing about all the great times Daddy and I had shared. I relived the Pirate games we'd gone to together. I remembered standing and cheering together when we went to the Pittsburgh Steelers' training camp at St. Vincent College in Latrobe, Pennsylvania.

One year we were in Latrobe going to our car when I noticed a guy in the parking lot who looked familiar. I asked, "Daddy? Is that a Pittsburgh Steeler?"

"Yes, honey, I think you're right," he replied.

Today, no matter how hard I try, I can't remember which Steeler it was. He must have heard us talking about him because he looked over and waved to us. Daddy was sure surprised to find out that I knew who the players were when they weren't wearing their team uniforms.

I recalled every camping trip. He took me to Girl Scout meetings and events. I loved it when he took me to the coal mine where he worked. Dad's buddies used to say to him, "I see you have your boss with you today."

With a great big smile on his face, his chest swelling with pride and his head held high, he always replied, "I sure do." Even though it was all in fun, it made me feel like the most important girl in the world every time.

Every April we sat side by side in front of the TV and gave loud advice to the teams during the annual NFL draft. Sometimes they would have been better off listening to us.

Daddy taught me innumerable things: how to fish, change a tire, change the oil in the car. I learned all about cars and tools from Daddy. I was a happy tomboy.

One time Mom caught him teaching me how to use a circular saw. She went ballistic. As soon as she was out of sight, Dad turned to me with a grin that erupted into a laugh and said, "You know your mom just has to worry."

In between gales of laughter, I replied, "I know."

Then we went back to using the saw.

These were just a few of the happy times that Daddy and I shared on my way to being a woman.

In April of 2001, the doctors gave us the greatest news that any family could receive. They said my daddy had beaten cancer. Everyone was delirious with happiness. Except me. That damn premonition hung over me like a psychic storm cloud of gloom. I tried to force myself to be happy. Maybe the premonition was wrong.

I prayed, "God, please let it be wrong."

Finally, finally I convinced myself that I'd been wrong. I was able to be really and truly happy. My dad had survived cancer! I was never so happy to be wrong.

Now Daddy would be able to go camping with

Jeremy and teach him how to bait a hook and catch fish. He could spoil him, play catch, and do all those things that make a grandpa so special. They'd be able to go to ball games together. Daddy would watch Jeremy play, grow, and become a young man.

Tears of relief cascaded down my face and just wouldn't stop.

Two weeks later, he was admitted to the hospital. The diagnosis: inoperable, incurable cancer. The battle was over. At 3:00 a.m., he suffered a stroke. At 3:00 p.m., as his favorite daytime program (*Days of Our Lives*) came on the air on Thursday, May 3, Daddy died. That was two days before my wedding anniversary. He was buried two days after it.

That damn premonition was true. I hated it! Whatever was happening to me, I HATED IT!

I've never told anyone until now, but I could sense that my dad knew he was dying when he was admitted to the hospital that final time. He resented missing the opportunity to spend more time with Jeremy. He was sad that he couldn't do those things he had dreamed of doing with his grandson. Then he suffered that damn stroke that even took away his last 12 hours.

I managed to ignore my psychic experiences for nearly a year. Maybe if I ignored them long enough and hard enough, they'd go away. I was so upset about my dad that I had no time for anything else, including dealing with my feelings. I blamed the doctors for giving everyone, including me, false hopes. I blamed God for taking my son's pap-pap before he really got to know him.

As time passed, I slowly let go of my anger. Usually that's healthy, but for me it seemed to bring back those weird experiences with a vengeance. After a year's respite, I was seeing and hearing scary things all over again.

I even cried out loud, "Why are these things happening again? Why me?"

I was determined to ignore them. Well, that didn't work. *Everything* started back up again. I was frustrated beyond frustration. I woke in the middle of the night having indecipherable flashes of information. I couldn't get back to sleep. I'd spend the rest of the night trying to figure out what they meant.

Phase Three: A Glimmering

A Psychic and "Paranormal Activity"

    One day my cousin Kristina mentioned a psychic reading. Could this help me? I had to know more. I got the psychic's contact information, but I hesitated. Should I do this? All these things had been happening to me for all these years and I just couldn't explain it. Could I get them to stop? I had questions I needed answers to. But did I have to go to a psychic to get them?
    All my life I have been a Christian. I was taught from an early age not to believe in psychics, fortune tellers, and so on. God is the answer to all questions. People who try to do what only He can do, like see the future, are sinful. I didn't want to go against everything I had been taught, but I couldn't take much more of my life as it was. I needed help. What would my husband say?

I made up my mind I was going to the psychic. Then that streak of white light appeared again. Even though we passed it off as nothing more than car headlights, it solidified my decision to see the psychic. I prayed for God to forgive me. I'm not preaching my religion to you, but for years I had been praying for this burden to be lifted, or at least explained. Maybe, just maybe, pointing me toward the psychic was God's way of answering my prayers.

She gave me what I consider a fairly accurate reading. I told her about my visions, premonitions, and other experiences. She told me that I am very sensitive and empathetic. I thought, *She's right. I am a very sensitive person, and I take things to heart.* My feelings do get hurt quite easily at times. And sometimes I feel what people are going through as if it were happening to me. Having sympathy for others is great, but empathy can be painful.

The reading came to a conclusion, but I still didn't know what was happening to me.

And my experiences didn't stop. If anything, they increased in both frequency and power. I couldn't even talk with my preacher. I was afraid he would say I was possessed.

Then John, Jeremy, and I pulled up stakes and moved again. We moved in with my mother in a double-wide in Mt. Pleasant, Pennsylvania, my hometown. It was a new start, and maybe all this crap would stop. The double-wide had no upstairs, so at least I wouldn't be hearing footsteps on the stairs at night. It wasn't much reassurance, but I took what I could get.

A week after we moved in, the radio woke me up during the night. But there wasn't any radio playing. I went all through the house and made sure of that. I did find that my son had fallen asleep with the TV on. I turned it off and went back to bed.

From that time on, I had an evening ritual. Before

going to bed, I checked on my son and turned his TV off if it was still on. Even so, every few nights, I would be awakened by that darn radio. Or I'd hear the mumbling of people talking, as if a loud party was going on somewhere. I had to get up in the morning to go to work, and I didn't appreciate having my sleep interrupted.

To add insult to injury, my husband and son slept right through all the noise. I thought that one of our neighbors must be playing their radio loud in the middle of the night and was determined to find out who. In a roundabout way, I asked all my neighbors if they had heard anything during the night. Nope, nobody heard a thing. Back to square one. I'd just try to ignore it. I asked my mom about the neighborhood. She said it was a quiet place, never noisy at night. So I put it on the back burner and minded my own business.

In the meantime, my mom told me that she had seen some previews of new shows coming on TV that looked really interesting.

"I'll watch them with you, Mom, just to see if I like them."

I was hooked! These were shows about ghost hunters, psychic detectives, hauntings, and other paranormal activity. (That was a new term for me: paranormal activity.) I couldn't wait for the next episodes to air. All the ghost stories seemed so intriguing and exotic – and familiar.

There was a show about people who wanted to learn more about paranormal happenings. They helped people who were afraid of the inexplicable things happening around them.

Watching these shows made me ask even more questions about my circumstances. To a person, the clients told the paranormal investigators that people would think they were crazy for pursuing the investigation. While we sat together watching the shows, I began to tell Mom that I knew what the people who asked for help were going through and that I feared people would think the same of me. Mom knew that I'd had some strange experiences. I'm sure she remembered my fear of her parents' house. But she continued to insist, "We don't talk about those kinds of things."

You see, Mom had to believe the paranormal was nonexistent no matter what she heard, saw, and felt. To do otherwise would be to go against everything that her religion and upbringing taught her. Belief in the occult was *sinful*. Any strange experiences she or I had lived through just had to have a rational explanation. That explanation might not be available yet, but it was there somewhere and would make its presence known at the proper time.

The paranormal team always reassured their clients that they weren't crazy at all. The things they were seeing and hearing (and smelling) were real, and sometimes the investigators could prove that. I really wanted to get in touch with those investigators. It finally dawned on me that I wasn't alone. There were many, many people out there experiencing the same things. Maybe I wasn't crazy after all! I had the first glimmerings of hope.

Then the footsteps started again. I heard footsteps in the front of the house, so I went out to the living room to see who had come in. Only there was nobody there. I went outside to see if anybody had come in and gone out again. No such luck. I blamed it on my overactive imagination.

When it got dark, I closed and latched all the windows, locked the doors, and shut off the computer and such. Jeremy went to his room for the night. I was planning to enjoy a little me time in front of the TV before turning in.

Footsteps again! It had to be either my mother or my hubby coming home from work early. I went to see. The door was still locked and no cars were in the driveway.

Oh, my God, someone must have broken in! It was déjà *vu* all over again. That night in the cabin when the burglary took place rushed back into my consciousness. It was happening all over again!

I rushed from room to room and closet to closet in a frantic state, checking the whole house. My boy was sleeping the sleep of innocence, undisturbed. I made sure his window was locked and his closet was empty. I checked our bedroom, the den, the bathroom, the hall closet, and my mother's room, closet, and bathroom.

There was no intruder. What a relief! But even so, I was so worked up that I couldn't sleep that night. And it happened on a weekend when both Mom and John were working night shifts. I didn't tell either of them because I didn't want to be ridiculed for my imagination.

The next time I heard the footsteps, I wasn't alone, and I wasn't the only one hearing them. Jeremy was playing in his room and I was watching TV with John in our bedroom. We thought it was Mom coming home from work, and we went to the kitchen to greet her. Her car wasn't in the driveway.

"John," I asked, "did you hear those footsteps?"

"Uh-huh," he replied. "Wasn't it your mother coming home?"

"No, John. She's not home yet."

Hmmm, so I wasn't the only one hearing footsteps. By now they were happening day and night. Mom said that she heard them in the middle of the night right outside her bedroom door. She thought it was me getting up for work. (Some days I had to get up as early as 3:30 a.m.) Or she thought someone was walking to the bathroom. She claimed she thought nothing of it.

The sounds escalated. I heard kitchen cabinet doors being slammed open and closed. I had no idea why somebody would be making so much noise in the kitchen at night. I went looking for my mom to see if she needed help finding something. I found her quietly reading a book. She said, "I thought it was one of you. I wondered why you were being so loud."

I said, "It wasn't me. Or John. Or Jeremy."

She gave me a strange look and returned to reading her book.

"What next?" I asked myself. And I got my answer. We started hearing the front door open, then close, all on its own. We tried to pretend that it was someone coming in and going right back out, but we knew better. It was happening too often.

As the little girl in *Poltergeist* said, "They're baack."

One day I was in my bedroom watching TV when my mother called me from the kitchen. I got up and went to the kitchen to see if she wanted help unloading groceries from her car. But there was no one there. I went to hold the door open for her, but she wasn't even home yet. I was worried, so I called her cell phone. She told me that she was still at the store but was getting ready to call me to ask if I would meet her at the door and help her carry the groceries in. I couldn't explain it and didn't try.

A Dream?

Around that time, I had the strangest dream. At least I *think* it was a dream. I have never experienced anything like it. It marked a turning point in my life.

I saw myself in a long white summer dress walking barefoot toward a bright light of the purest white. Even though it was the purest, brightest white light I had ever seen, it didn't hurt my eyes. I walked right into it, feeling no fear. I stepped into the most beautiful summer day. A slight breeze ruffled my long brown hair while the beams of the sun warmed my face.

No painter could have captured the perfection of this day. I looked around and found myself in a field of yellow daisies surrounded by verdant green. This field led down to a large, serene lake reflecting the mountains beyond, topped by a gorgeous blue sky speckled with puffy white cottony clouds.

It was indescribably relaxing, the most peaceful atmosphere that I have ever been in. That's about the best I can describe it. It was more of a feeling than a sense of place.

My dad came to me and said, "It's not your time yet. Go back."

"I don't understand, Daddy. I don't want to leave this peaceful place."

"It's not your time. Go back," he insisted.

I finally realized what he meant. Although I was safe in that comforting, warm, peaceful place, I had to go back to the physical world because there were still things I needed to do. I called out to God and begged him to let me go back. "I can't leave my husband and son alone yet. It's too early to leave them. They *need* me!"

Instantly, I woke up in my own bed feeling that I would be all right. As I tried to recapture the experience, I fell asleep again. Next thing I knew, the alarm clock announced morning.

I will never forget the warm feeling of that beautiful place. What started as a dream became an unforgettable experience of enlightenment.

A Visit from My Dad

A few days later, while crossing the living room, I heard someone call my name as though he were standing right at my ear. I couldn't identify the voice other than to be sure it wasn't my dad.

"Beverly," said a distinctly male voice. Before I could spin around to catch whoever was sneaking up on me, I felt two hands push on my shoulders hard enough to make me lose my footing. I caught myself, regained my balance, and turned around, only to find myself alone. Whoever pushed me had disappeared in an instant. I neither saw nor sensed him now. And our home's open floor plan would have allowed me to see anyone near me. Whoever it was, I treated him to a couple of unladylike words.

Soon after that, in the middle of October 2005 my sister got married. At her reception, I was standing alone at a table she had set up in memory of our dad. I picked up one of his pictures and looked directly into his eyes, wishing that he could be there to see Sis on her wedding day.

"Beverly," a different voice said right behind me.

I cried out, "Daddy! You're here!" as I turned around. I was so happy to hear my dad's voice again.

Then I realized where I was and looked about to see if anybody had noticed. I was so upset when I remembered that my dad had passed on, I started to cry. But at least I could tell my sister that Daddy had come to her wedding reception.

I'd have to figure out how to tell her. You know, "We don't talk about those kinds of things." I hoped she wouldn't be too afraid. I thought she'd probably be so happy to know Daddy was at her wedding that she wouldn't care about anything else.

I just knew that he was having a grand old time,

toasting the newlyweds with "root beer," a family joke. You see, we used to camp at a private campground that banned alcoholic beverages. Dad liked a beer before retiring for the night, so he'd pour some into a big cup and call it "root beer." Ever after, when Dad asked for a beer, I'd say, "You mean root beer."

As autumn transposed into winter, the footsteps in my house were no longer in another room or down the hall. They were much closer. They came right up on me.

Was I losing my mind? Was I imagining the footsteps? Here's the real kicker: all the floors in our house were carpeted, except for the kitchen! How could I hear footsteps on carpeting? If all this sounds confusing to you, just imagine how I felt.

One day after lunch I was in the kitchen doing dishes. John and Jeremy were in another part of the house. I both heard and felt someone walking behind me. I thought it might be Jeremy coming up behind me to startle me. Or maybe John sneaking up behind me to give me a hug. I didn't care which of my favorite two people in the world it was.

"Hey, what would you like to do for the rest of the day?" I asked. There was no answer, just the feeling of weight shifting on the floor.

Turning around, I asked, again, "What would you like to do for the rest of the day?"

I was alone in the kitchen with whoever or whatever was treading on the floor. But not for long. Both John and Jeremy came into the kitchen, asking me what I had wanted as though they had heard the question for the first time.

Soon after the kitchen episode, John and I were watching TV in our room late one night when, all of a sudden, a streak of pure white light moved across two walls of the room. This time it was in the center of the walls, in a place no outside light could reach.

Besides, the only window in the room faces a utility shed that blocks all the light. And the venetian blinds were closed with the drapes drawn.

It couldn't be a reflection from the TV because the light appeared on the same wall as the TV. It just didn't make sense. We had no idea what was going on or what to do about it, but it was getting harder and harder to deny the evidence of our senses.

Right after the unexplained encounter with the streak of light, my mom told me about another show on TV, this time with a paranormal team from Pennsylvania. Their headquarters is only a few hours away. This show differs from the other in that the team works in conjunction with a psychic/medium. We love this show now.

Mom likes to watch to see what explanation is given for these so-called paranormal happenings. She always looks for the "logical explanation." And, whenever the psychic/medium on the show is able to verify what the client is experiencing,

Mom always says that it's because the psychic has been briefed on the situation and told what kind of paranormal activity is expected. She says that they never tell us what's been going on off-camera.

I watch it because I am in tune with the psychic/medium. When we watched the show together, I amazed Mom by telling her what was going to happen.

"Is this a rerun?" she would ask.

"I don't think so. How could it be a rerun if it's the first show of the season?"

"Did you see it earlier, or maybe see a preview?"

"No, Mom, I never saw any of it before."

"Then how in the world do you know what's going to happen next?"

I told Mom that what she was watching on TV had

happened to me. And she opened up, just a little, to tell me about things that had happened to her. We would talk a little, but then she would clam up again.

Mom was raised to believe that anybody who believed in these things was influenced by the devil. She reads the Bible every night before going to bed. She thought I should seek advice from a minister or some kind of cleric. I told her that I have prayed to God to take away these things that disturb me so deeply. I tried going to church every Sunday and praying for God's intercession, but it didn't work. I was at my wits' end.

A Titanic Visit

As the summer of 2008 drew to a close we wanted to do something out of the ordinary to remember it. The *Tribune-Review* had an article featuring the *Titanic* artifacts display at the Carnegie Science Center in Pittsburgh. We decided to go: Mom, Jeremy, Sis, my niece, and me.

The *Titanic*, its disaster, and all the mythos and stories surrounding it have intrigued me since I first heard about it. I don't fully understand my interest in it. After all it was such a horrific event surrounded with sadness. Nonetheless, I wanted to learn all I could about it and the causes of its sinking.

We drove to Pittsburgh, parked the car, and entered the building. In order to add to the realism of Titanic – The Artifacts, each of us was treated as a passenger on that fateful journey. I received a boarding pass from the White Star Line giving me permission to board the *RMS Titanic*.

The other side of the boarding pass, which was actually my ticket to enter the exhibit, had detailed information. This included the name of the ship, its port of embarkation, and the date April 10, 1912. Next came the name of the passenger who originally held that boarding pass. It gave the name, age, country of origin, and traveling associates. The class being traveled in was listed next, along with the cabin number, and the passenger's final destination. Next was the biographical information available on that passenger, including their reason for taking the trip.

It was all designed to make the experience as realistic as possible. I have to admit that I was completely enthralled. I was eager to enter, but we had to wait while a small group ahead of us "embarked." While we waited, we were given a small hand-held device, like an MP3 player, that would explain the artifacts as we toured.

Finally, we passed behind the black curtain that shielded the entrance and went back in history to another time. Hundreds of items that were recovered from the actual resting place of the legendary *Titanic* were on display for my examination. Something, I didn't know what, drew me inexorably to this exhibition.

I wasn't sure what to expect, but I certainly didn't expect the mood that permeated the exhibit. Sure, displays that contained pictures and items from the Titanic were there for my scrutiny, but it was the ambience of the room that got to me. The atmosphere turned somber and the air felt heavy with sadness. There was just so much to see and read. But I was so overwhelmed with emotions that I had to sit down to try to absorb it all. Horrible isn't a strong enough word to describe what the victims of this great tragedy went through.

One display was of a crew member 's uniform: shirt, jacket, pants. They looked *so* small that I felt it must be a child's. Was it a young cabin boy, sailing to his death? Another case held a lady's hairbrush. It was display after display emanating melancholy and loss: paper money, cups, silverware, and clothing. Too much to take in all at once.

A trunk had been recovered intact. I examined it for any markings that would give a clue as to its owner - not that it would make any difference to either of us.

Next I was faced with actual pieces of the ship that had been raised up from the ocean floor 12,415 below. Another display was interactive. It was designed to demonstrate how cold the iceberg that sank the ship was. You were instructed to place your hands on that display and experience the chill of the waters of the North Atlantic at 2:20 a.m. on April 15, 1912.

I tried, I really tried. But I just couldn't leave my hands in contact with that display for any length of time. I started feeling extremely uncomfortable. I can't explain that feeling other than that: *uncomfortable*. I got away from there and went to the next area.

It depicted recreations of the different class accommodations on the ocean liner. One room was decorated with red walls, so naturally I called it the Red Room. It was a stateroom reserved for first-class passengers. It was equipped with a bed, a small table, and two chairs.

I found my gaze concentrating on one seat for some reason. Gradually a woman wearing a red outfit topped with a large wide-brimmed hat appeared sitting at the table, daintily sipping tea from a small porcelain cup. Even though I could see her sipping, I couldn't make out her face. Then she faded into nothingness as gradually as she had appeared, leaving behind a definite aura of substantiation about me.

I stood transfixed until my son tugged at me and pulled me along to the next display. I felt that there was more to come, but Jeremy's interruption broke the connection.

As we proceeded through the exhibit, I got the impression of a shadow flitting nearby that was blacker than the darkness in that area. I couldn't be sure, but it did cause me to feel somewhat off-balance.

I was sure, however, about the spirits who were now walking around and through the exhibit. I was thankful they were not trying to communicate. That would have been too overwhelming for me to handle. They were just empty reflections or imprints of the past. Paranormal investigators call that a residual haunting. This one was a classic example.

We wended our way to the end of the exhibition. It was time for us to go. The spirits did not follow us into the last room we encountered, which was filled with passenger and crew lists. The passengers were listed by class and whether or not they survived. Even though the premise of the room was a sad one, it felt lighter for me. My equilibrium returned to normal as I left the sphere of influence of the spirits.

I desperately yearned to learn more, but I had had about as much spirit propinquity as I could handle for one day. I wanted to rush outside into the fresh air of the warm, sunny afternoon. But first I paused to remember 2,222 people as their ship sank into the North Atlantic on an icy April night.

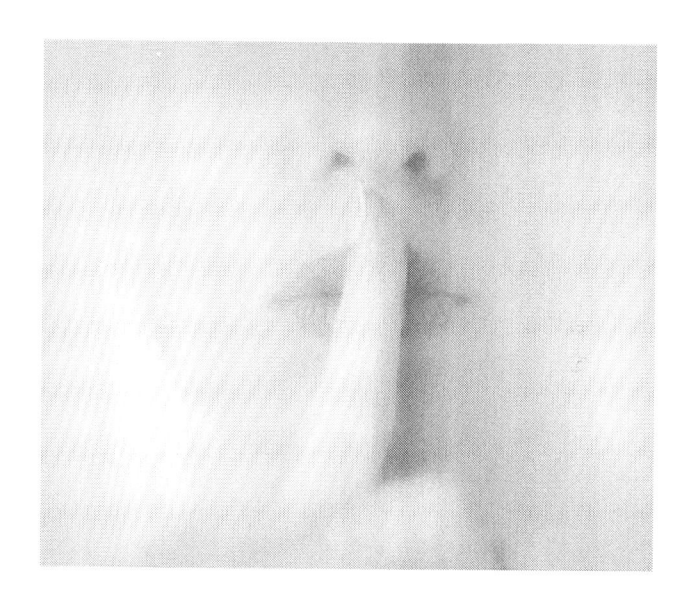

Phase Four: A Breakthrough ... Maybe

My Introduction to Paranormal Investigation

The next time Mom and I watched our favorite paranormal TV show, I decided to contact the psychic/medium featured on the show, who happened to be Catholic. To my dismay, I learned that he works only with children. If I wanted to ask questions of him, I would have to pay for a private reading. That was way beyond my resources, so I just continued to watch his show and glean what I could from it.

Before long, he got his own show, where he helped children with their paranormal experiences. He probably didn't know it, but he was helping me as well. I was learning a great deal about my own experiences. Oh, how I wished I could have had someone to help me understand what was happening when I was their age!

The only advice I ever got from my mother and grandmother was, "We don't talk about those kinds of things." Of course, they wouldn't have let me talk to him when I was growing up anyway. If I ever get the chance, I'll give that psychic a great big hug and my sincere thanks.

Time passed. I often saw black shadowy forms going into and coming out of the bathroom, then entering one of the bedrooms and disappearing. It was about time John and I had a talk about these things and what had been happening. All this time, John had thought that I was just fascinated by the paranormal. It was past time to set him straight.

I started by telling him about my grandparents' house. I told him all about the specter of a man, the sinister laugh, the sense of someone watching, watching me, even when the house was supposed to be empty. I explained that overall feeling of fear I would get whenever I got near the place. Then I sat back and waited for John's response.

"I'm really glad the deal on the house didn't go through, then," he said.

"Me, too." I plowed on. I explained that I watch those ghost shows on TV because some of the events depicted have actually happened to me.

John didn't say much. Since he is a practical, show-me kind of a guy, I guess he didn't know what to say. He's the kind of a skeptic who doesn't believe it if he can't understand it. He's seen and heard some unexplainable things himself, but he won't admit it.

For instance, one time we were watching a TV program when a black shadow walked into our bedroom. Aghast, I asked if he had seen it. "Yep," he said. Then he went back to watching the TV show.

Sometimes I tried to talk with him about it.

He'd say, "Bev, it's your thing, not mine."

One night we were sound asleep in bed. It was

sometime after midnight during the silent hours. There was not even a car on the road. Suddenly someone grabbed my feet and shook them. I immediately thought it was Jeremy waking me to tell me he'd had a nightmare. I raised my head, but there was nobody there. My husband slept on in our bed and Jeremy was sound asleep in his room.

A couple of nights later I awoke to find a black shadowy entity standing near the head of my bed watching me. As soon as I was fully awake, it disappeared. It startled me so much that my actions even awakened my husband.

"What's the matter?" he muttered.

I answered, "Nothing. Just a bad dream."

I couldn't tell him that I'd been startled awake by a black shadow staring at me. It sounded crazy even to me. I tried to tell myself that maybe it *was* just a bad dream. In any case, I've never seen that particular shadow again.

One day my mother showed me an article in the paper that she said might be fun to do and just might give me some answers. I agreed.

I asked John, "What do you think? Mind if I look into this?"

He simply said, "If it helps you, babe, go ahead and have fun."

Halloween was just around the corner, and the article was about a local property owner who has special events for Halloween at the Lonesome Valley Farms across from the Westmoreland County Fairgrounds. That year he made arrangements with the Society for Paranormal Investigations, Research, Ideas and Theories of Southwestern Pennsylvania (SPIRITswp) to conduct an investigation on his property. The public was invited to meet the team, learn how they conduct investigations, and maybe even take part. Mom and I decided to go.

We got to talk with the founder of the team, Barry

Brudnak, and he showed us some of the equipment they use in their investigations. Both Mom and I had a ton of questions, but I had to be careful what I said. Remember, Mom likes to tell herself that she's a skeptic; she's also a very religious person. Also, this was the first time I met Mr. Brudnak, and I don't share my experiences with just anybody. I'm sure by now you understand why.

He did seem to be trustworthy and he was extremely interested in what I had to say, so I decided to tell him some of what I'd seen and felt. Just a bit, not enough to scare my mom or make him think I was unhinged. He asked us to stay for the investigation that night. Mom was willing, so we stayed. I think she was secretly interested but didn't want to say so, if you get my drift.

I was excited to be part of a paranormal investigation, if only as an observer.

Lonesome Valley Farms is a large tract of land next to the fairgrounds. Every Halloween the centerpiece is a huge bonfire. Nearby is a refreshment stand featuring fried Oreos, along with other tasty tidbits. A real crowd pleaser is the pumpkin sling, a giant slingshot that uses pumpkins for ammunition. The target is a car set out in the field. I for one am happy that I have nothing to do with cleaning up the car afterward.

A haunted hayride is available for the more adventurous folks. Realistic props are located throughout the entire area. Volunteers dress up as maniacal chainsaw murderers, zombies, ghosts, and so on.

Every year, something special is added. This year it was the investigation by SPIRITswp. I had already decided to sit quietly and say nothing.

Those of us lucky enough to go on the actual investigation climbed aboard a wagon that took us out to the area of psychic interest. Once we arrived, we were told to remain aboard the wagon for several reasons related to safety. (It was dark. We were in the middle of a cornfield. They didn't want anybody to get hurt. Something about insurance.)

Barry started out by explaining the purpose and operation of each piece of equipment. A device called a K II meter was handed around. It has five lights in a row that light up sequentially as it detects an electromagnetic field or energy passing in front of it. The green pilot light is always on when the device is on. As the strength of the field in front of the K II increases, the lights turn on in order from the pilot to another green, then yellow, then orange, and finally red.

At our outdoor location, away from power lines and radio sources, there should be no reading on the K II, and there wasn't.

While the K II was being passed around, Barry demonstrated another device, the electromagnetic field (EMF) meter. Its digital display shows the surrounding EMF level at any given time. As the strength of the field changes, it shows the amount of the change. This device also shows if something passes in front of it that disturbs the base level of the field.

Finally, Barry explained the hand-held digital audio recorder. It is used to pick up voices and noises that human ears are not attuned to. It is so sensitive that it can pick up the sound of skin rubbing against it when it is handled.

Barry explained that, after an investigation is completed, the contents of the audio recorder are downloaded into a computer. All the members of SPIRITswp don headphones and listen to every second of the recordings for EVPs (electronic voice phenomena), evidence of paranormal communication that can be heard only through the playback of digital recording devices.

These three instruments and several others not being used on this particular investigation collect evidence of paranormal activity. All the evidence is evaluated by members of the team, and the results of the investigation are given to the clients to help them deal with what kind of activity is taking place around them.

As a matter of professional ethics, SPIRITswp never charges for its services. Donations are accepted for the purchase of new equipment and other items that help conduct investigations.

Barry asked questions of and fielded questions from the other observers, trying to get responses from the spirits, haunts, ghosts, or whoever was there in the paranormal plane.

I began to see images and hear things as well. The psychic/medium was in our group. She was telling the group what she was picking up on. Later, I realized that I was nodding my head in agreement because I was picking up on those same things—as well as some that she didn't mention.

Barry noticed me nodding, so he started asking me questions about what I was hearing and seeing. My mom also had a question that she wanted to ask me, but she didn't. I knew what she was thinking: She wanted to know if Dad was with us. I answered, "No."

After the investigation, the wagon headed back to the drop-off point. As we jostled along, I was looking around and enjoying the way the area had been decorated for Halloween.

One prop in particular caught my eye due to its realism. It was a little girl about six or seven years old dressed in a white nightgown, all ready for bed. It was especially realistic, spooky, and unsettling

"Hey, there," I called out to one of the volunteer workers who escorted us in the wagon.

"Back at ya," he replied with a smile. "What can I do for you?"

"That prop of the little girl in a nightgown is a perfect

touch to add to the eeriness of this area. And so realistic! If I didn't know better, I'd have thought she was real. I just wanted to compliment you on the effect."

His smile was replaced with a frown of confusion as he replied, "I'm not sure what you're talking about. We don't have any props this far from the main activity."

"Of course you do," I told him, turning back and pointing where I had just seen her. "She's right over there."

But she was gone. She had vanished into thin air.

The incident and the memory of that little girl's long straight hair cascading down her back left me feeling unsettled for some time afterward.

Barry asked me to keep in touch with him and invited me to join the group. I told him I'd think about it.

When I got home that night, my mind was a jumble of conflicting ideas and feelings. I wasn't sure of anything at that point. I had a ton of new information to sift through and two tons of new questions.

On the one hand, if I joined the group, I'd have to attend meetings. I'd have to try to get my work schedule arranged to accommodate them. And, since we had only one car, I wasn't about to ask John to schedule his work around paranormal group meetings. What would Mom and the rest of the family think? There hadn't been a wellspring of support coming from that corner. Most of all, what about my own beliefs?

On the other hand, Barry and his team don't look at me as some strange creature. They're like me. They're genuinely interested in what I've been through. They accept me for who and what I am, without judging me.

They believe me and take my experiences seriously. Finally, for the first time in my life, I had people I could talk openly with about what has been happening to me all my life.

What a relief! I had actually found people willing to listen to me and possibly even help me. I wasn't crazy after

We Don't Talk About Those Kinds of Things

all! That was a real light at the end of a very long tunnel.

I started praying even more than before to find out which life path was mine to take. I spoke with the pastor of my church, phrasing my questions very carefully.

I asked him what I hoped he would accept as a rhetorical question, but I think he saw through my subterfuge.

I asked, "If, in our faith, we are not to believe in such things as fortune tellers and psychics, then what do I do if I am one?"

He said that he didn't know the answer but would consult his superiors. He would tell them that an anonymous member of the church had discovered that she had some abilities, and she didn't know what to do about them.

A few weeks later I got my answer. My pastor's superiors, after conferring and praying over it, suggested that I get an MRI and a CT scan of my head. If those tests came back normal, I should come talk to them again to see what could be done. I was shocked and mortified. I despaired of getting any help from that quarter.

When I could talk again, I spoke as if I was actually considering his proposal.

I said, "How am I supposed to go to my doctor and ask for these tests without sounding crazy? Especially since my insurance company probably won't cover it without a proper diagnosis." I felt that my faith had just been challenged.

While my faith in God remained strong, I lost faith in my church. I prayed that I would lose my abilities. Or that I would be shown a way to use them to help people.

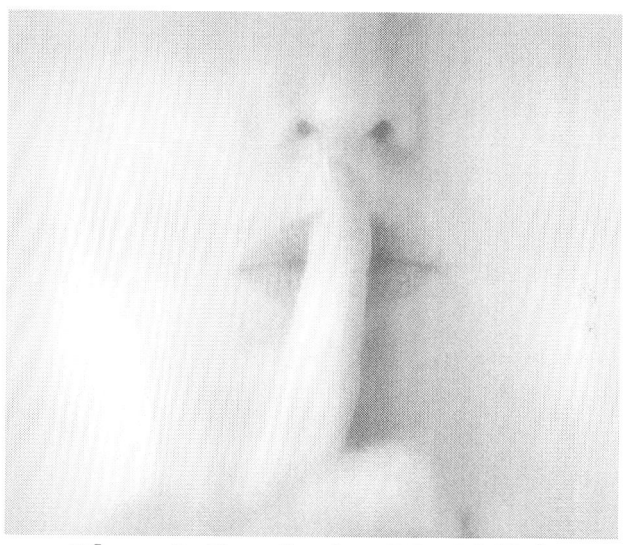

Phase 5: Developing My Abilities

I Learn Not to Ignore My Visions

    Two weeks later I got an answer to my prayers. My mother, my sister, and I went shopping. While reaching for something on a shelf, my mom got a scratch on her arm. Just a little one that gave up a few drops of blood, nothing serious. But when she showed it to me, I was suddenly flooded with information and visions.
    No longer was I in the store with my mother and sister. I was transported out to the parking lot, where I found myself next to an older lady. She was a few inches shorter than I, and her luxuriously long gray hair cascaded all the way down her back. She wore a green jacket over an ankle-length denim skirt. She stood there in a daze, holding a hankie to the right side of her head to stem the blood flow from a wound. She had fallen in the lot, striking the right side of her head. A kind person helped her to the customer service desk.

In the blink of an eye I was back in the store shopping as though nothing had happened. I kept my vision, precognition, whatever you want to call it, to myself.

Ten minutes later we went through the checkout. As we were leaving the store, the woman I had seen in my vision, wearing the same clothing I had seen, came in. She was clutching a blood-stained hankie to the right side of her face. She said she had fallen in the parking lot a few minutes earlier, striking the right side of her face. Had I paid proper attention to my vision, I might have been able to prevent her injury. That was when I knew I was supposed to use my abilities to help people. It would be wrong to lose them.

I Become a Paranormal Investigator

I got back in touch with Barry Brudnak of SPIRITswp. Barry said that, before I could join, I would have to become a certified paranormal investigator (CPI). It would be a complicated, arduous venture, so I waited until all the hullabaloo of the Christmas season was over.

Then I enrolled in the online courses and embarked on a new phase of my life. The courses covered all aspects of paranormal investigating and were a great preparation for the test. My next hurdle was the test itself. The CPI test is comprehensive and challenging, and it has a time limit of two hours from start to finish. As if that weren't enough pressure, you get only three tries to pass it.

The test is crammed with questions about investigative procedures, equipment for paranormal research and its uses, what constitutes valid visual and auditory evidence, and all the necessary standardized paperwork. The last part of the exam was a mock mini-investigation. I had to fill out and submit all the forms, showing I had followed all the proper steps in my investigation.

The wait began. I was on pins and needles worrying about the outcome of the test. Ten minutes at a computer may not seem long to you, but it was the longest ten minutes of my life.

When notified of the results, I was devastated. While I hadn't failed the exam, I hadn't scored high enough to become a CPI. I would have to retake the test. The second time around I scored high enough and became an official Certified Paranormal Investigator. I like the way the sound of it rolls off my tongue, especially after all that hard work.

I was welcomed into the SPIRITswp Team and started attending the weekly meetings. I can't express how good it felt to be a member of a team where I could share my experiences and learn more about psychic experiences, paranormal events, and my abilities. Soon I was able to acquire my own equipment, which I still use today.

There is one unusual thing about that equipment and me. When I am using and monitoring the equipment, it prevents me from picking up psychic events with my own inherent abilities. I can't do both at the same time.

Luckily, my work schedule allowed me to attend the meetings. It just took a bit of maneuvering to get there. I would have to drive John to work and leave Jeremy with Mom while I used our car. So far, so good.

Sometimes I had to borrow Mom's car while John took ours. And once in a while it meant that John would borrow Mom's car while I took ours. Then the rare occasion happened when I took our car and Mom dropped John off using her car. Confused? Think how I felt.

As I got more involved in the team, I felt more comfortable sharing my experiences with them. What a relief that they believed me! It felt as if a dam had burst. As I was more and more able to share with other members of the group, my abilities grew.

I still didn't understand what the sensory input was all about, so I talked with Barry to get his insight. I hoped that he could figure out how to use my abilities. Thankfully, he was willing to spend the time with me and help me build confidence in myself and my abilities.

I finally got to participate in my first investigation. It was at the same place where I'd met the team. This time the roles were reversed, and it felt great!

After a year, I'd come a long way. Barry assured me that I was truly a psychic/medium, but I just wasn't sure. I no longer denied that I had some abilities, but I was having trouble with the title, though I'm not sure why.

I could do the things that a psychic/medium does, so maybe the title fit. Was it that I was afraid of being called a demon or a devil worshiper? Would I be taken seriously or ridiculed? I couldn't go through that.

I decided I wouldn't call myself a psychic/medium. All I knew was that I wanted to help people. The best way I could do that was to keep doing what I was doing without people knowing what I was. So I continued with the team.

When the NCAA Basketball Tournament called March Madness came around that year, my husband and I had a friendly competition as we both tried to pick the winners of the 64 teams all the way to the final. John picks his teams by their records; I pick my teams randomly. I had picked the winner six out of the past eight seasons.

John laughs at me because I can pick a team to win and I have never watched a basketball game.

I have the same kind of luck (a.k.a. intuition) with the Super Bowl. I had picked the champions five out of the past eight years. I am a true Pittsburgh Steelers fan, so I cheer for them every time, even when I know they won't win. Too bad I can't pick lottery numbers like that. It's not for lack of trying, either.

My senses seem to have gotten quite a bit sharper since I've been with the team. And I seem to have become a lightning rod for paranormal activity. For instance, at home I've been seeing both black and white shadows. I've been hearing footsteps and doors opening and closing. I hear spirits talking and have had my name called many times when there was nobody else around. I get precognitive visions.

One day I was getting ready to take a shower. I got a fresh towel and washcloth and set them at the foot of my bed. I turned away to put something on the dresser, and when I turned back, the washcloth was at the head of the bed and the towel was opened. I was alone in the room, and anybody who walked in would have had to go around me to get to the bed.

Shortly thereafter, when I was walking from the kitchen to the dining room, a faint voice called out, "Hey." I paid it no mind. Maybe I hadn't really heard it. But that entity was not about to be denied. Two hands pushed me on the back to trip me as I walked away, not hard enough to make me fall, just enough to make me stumble. It was almost like tripping over my own feet. The entity didn't seem to be evil or harmful. It just wanted to get my attention. Then, satisfied that its existence had been noted, it left.

I continued to participate in investigations with the team and got the validation that I needed. It was important to the team and even more important to me to have proof that I really could communicate with spirits. I no longer worried about what people who didn't understand would think of me. I knew the truth.

We Don't Talk About Those Kinds of Things

I Psychically Witness a Murder

In 2010, all over the news were reports about a woman who had gone missing. As soon as I saw her picture in the newspaper, I was mentally blasted with bits and pieces of information about her and her circumstances that went together like a puzzle to form a horrible portrait of the anguish this poor young woman was going through.

Then she was murdered. I had never even imagined the awful things I was seeing. I knew how many people were involved in her murder and how many were men and how many were women.

I was afraid to take my conclusions to the authorities. How in the world could I walk into a police station and give detailed information about a current investigation, things only the guilty party would know outside the paranormal world?

They would conclude that I was either a murderer or a total nut case. I would wind up in a cell or a mental ward.

And I was lacking one bit of vital information: location. I knew *what* was happening, but I didn't know *where*.

The next day her battered body was found. The news reports confirmed everything that I already knew. I was shocked and deeply, deeply saddened.

I beat myself up over this girl's death. If only I had told someone, notified the authorities, done something.

Maybe she could have been saved. Right then and there I made up my mind: Never will I allow my fear of ridicule, rejection, or embarrassment to hold me back.

I was given this ability for a reason, and that reason was to help people. I vowed that that was exactly what I was going to do. This decision opened up the whole psychic world to me. I had removed the final barrier between me and my ability.

Communing with the Other Side

    I am now somewhat comfortable communicating with those on the spiritual plane. It's even kind of cool that I can talk to them without uttering a word. All I have to do is to think something, and they'll reply. The spirits' mouths don't open when they talk with me. It's all done telepathically. I can talk with them without anybody else knowing.
    Conversations with spirits were becoming an integral part of my life. The paranormal was constantly impinging on my psyche. I was surrounded by smells that nobody else could perceive.
    The smell of cigarette smoke permeated our bedroom, Jeremy's room, and the living room, even though no living person ever smoked anywhere in our home. Even though my dad had quit the habit before moving into the trailer. I never knew where it came from. I just knew that I didn't like the smell.
    The scent of vanilla pervaded the hallway that led to our bedrooms. It sometimes reached the living room as well. I didn't mind that aroma a bit. When I smelled bacon and freshly brewed coffee in the kitchen, I knew it was my dad. He was the only one to drink coffee in our household while he was alive. Strangely enough, those aromas appeared at four in the morning and again at nine at night.
    Though to some people they might have been unsettling, they actually comforted me. They reminded me of all those wonderful times I had spent with my daddy.
    My front door had a mind of its own. We heard it open and close so much that we started ignoring it. Even Jeremy heard it. One time about 4:30 a.m., he was awakened by the sound of someone coming in the front door. He told me that John was home from work. Good! That meant I could leave for my job without rushing for a change.

We Don't Talk About Those Kinds of Things

  Only it wasn't John; he didn't get home until later. And it couldn't have been my mom. She was still at work. Mom worked as an LPN in a nursing home on the night shift. Now I ignore the door and the footsteps until I actually see John when he gets home in the morning.
  I prayed that nobody would ever break in. With all the background noises we'd become used to, how would we know the difference between the usual phantoms and a burglar?
  When John and I sat at the dining room table and Jeremy played on his Wii game console in his bedroom, noises would come from the kitchen as though someone was rearranging the pots and pans.
  From where we sat, we could see into the kitchen, so we knew there was nobody in there. Sometimes it happened while we were sitting on the couch. We could see into the kitchen from there too. We got tired of checking on the noises and never finding anyone, so we just stopped worrying about them. They became part of our daily life.
  In the corner of the dining room was an old grandfather clock that we never turned on. One day, while I was sitting at the table with John reminiscing about my father, the pendulums and chains on the clock started moving on their own. The same thing happened with Mom too, only she was sitting in the living room when it happened.
  She later told me she was thinking about Dad at the time.
  One morning while I was in the kitchen, I heard someone call out my name. Mom was in the den working on the computer, so I went there.
  She asked, "What do you want?"
  I replied, "Nothing. I heard you call my name."
  "I heard *you* call *my* name," she said.
  I checked with Jeremy to see if he was calling, but he

said no. John wasn't yet home from work. Besides, it was definitely a woman's voice. As near as I could figure, it may have been my grandmother calling. I couldn't discern what she wanted.

My mom's favorite place to sit in the living room was a chair that, whenever someone reclined it, made a distinctive click. When I heard that click, I knew that Mom was in the chair, so I would walk in and chat with her. After the spirits began hanging out in our house, I can't count the number of times I heard that chair click, went in to talk to Mom, and found nobody there. The chair wouldn't even be reclined. I would turn and start walking away and I would hear that click again, as though someone was mocking me.

It finally irritated me to the point where I told the entity, "If you've got something to tell me, then just say it so I can hear you – or knock it off!" The clicking ceased. I waited for a minute and nothing happened, so I just went back to what I was doing.

My son woke up one night at midnight and came to me. "The noises from the kitchen. They scare me," he said. "Will you stay with me until I fall asleep?" Of course I did.

Another night I was standing just inside his bedroom doorway when he saw something standing behind me that terrified him so much he couldn't even tell me what it was. I spun on my heels but saw nothing. That is, I saw nothing with my eyes. My feelings told me that someone was there. Even if John hadn't been off work and catching up on some much-needed sleep, I would have known from the expression on Jeremy's face that it wasn't John. It was something or someone who frightened him.

It was, I decided, time for a talk. I was never going to tell my son, "We don't talk about those kinds of things."

I sat on the edge of Jeremy's bed and told him that he could talk to me about absolutely *anything*. I was there for him any time, day or night, and would take him seriously no matter what he had to say. There was no subject that could possibly be too weird or stupid for us to discuss.

"Okay," he answered, though he has never said anything further on the subject. He just keeps his door closed all the time and wants me to stay with him at night until he falls asleep.

Every so often Jeremy will ask me what I want when I haven't called him. I just tell him that it wasn't me, and he's fine with that.

But I still wanted to know what we were dealing with. I borrowed my mother's video camera and set it up to capture movement in most of the house outside the bedrooms. I set up a digital audio recorder as well, so I could listen for EVPs. I waited until everyone else had turned in for the night before turning on the devices. Then I went to bed.

Night after night I set up my paranormal surveillance system. Morning after morning, I checked for results.

On two occasions, I got electronic confirmation of my suspicions. Both times the video camera covered the living room, dining room, hallway, and bathroom door. Then, depending on how far to the right or left the camera was aimed, it covered either the back door or the door to the den.

The first anomaly was a pair of disembodied legs walking across the living room, accompanied by the sounds of footsteps creaking across the floorboards. At the same time, I could hear objects in the kitchen being loudly moved around on the counter tops. The cupboard doors could be heard opening and closing while pots and pans were being clanged against one another.

In the morning everything was undisturbed.

If the first instance was unusual, the second was truly bizarre. Again, I had set the camera on the corner of the kitchen counter. While it was recording, it was shaking and moving from side to side as though someone was doing it on purpose. But in order to touch the camera, a person would have to pass in front of the lens, thereby appearing on the tape. And nobody had been captured on the tape.

That same night, the digital voice recorder picked up my father's voice saying, "Hello."

"Mom?" I called. "Can you come in here for a minute?" Hearing that voice made me so happy that I couldn't wait.

"Sure, Bev, what do you want?" she asked. She came into the room and sat down.

All I said was, "Listen to this and tell me what you think." And I hit the "play" button.

She listened, her expression registering recognition and shock.

"Play it again," she asked.

I did, and when it got to the part where the voice on the recording said, "Hello," she said "Hello" back.

"Play it once more," she asked.

She listened to it for the third time and said, "It's Daddy."

"Yes Mom, it is Daddy. He's saying hello." That was about all I could say because my emotions were running away with me. Mom's voice was lost in her emotions as well. She had a smile of reminiscence on her face hearing her husband's voice after those nine long years since his passing.

When she gathered her wits about her again, she said, "You have to get your sister over here to listen to this and see what she has to say about it."

A couple of days later, when my sister listened to the recording, she too identified the voice as Daddy's, but she didn't have a smile on her face. She was totally creeped out.

My sister's reaction caused me to entertain a certain

We Don't Talk About Those Kinds of Things

amount of doubt about my methods. However, I did manage to sow a seed of understanding in my mother's mind. And when she watched parts of the videos that were made those nights, she couldn't offer any explanation of what she was seeing.

I made copies of the tapes and gave them to Barry. We were right in the middle of a paranormal investigation, but he said that he'd watch them later and tell me what he thought. He never did get back to me. I think he forgot about them.

Nevertheless, it was about time that Mama Grizzly had a heart-to-heart with whatever or whoever was frightening my son. I was not going to allow Jeremy to live in fear. I know all too well what that's like.

I said, "Whoever is bothering my son: please just leave him alone. He's young and doesn't understand. You're scaring him. So please just stop."

I guess politeness works. He wasn't bothered again for a good long time. The noises did continue, but they happened very early in the morning or very late at night when he was asleep. I know that it wasn't my dad because he was never that loud even when he was alive.

He was always so quiet around the house because Mom would sometimes fall asleep before going into work on the night shift, and he never got up in the middle of the night for no reason.

I can feel when my dad is around, though. He says hi or I see him out of the corner of my eye. He always, still, has a smile on his face. Sometimes I'll see his first name written, and I swear it looks just the way he used to sign his name. The smell of cigarettes, coffee, or bacon reminds me of him.

He doesn't come to me in dreams as much anymore unless he has to tell me something that is very important.

I've also seen someone who looks so much like my dad that I had to stare to make sure it wasn't him. Sure I know better, but for that minute it seemed to look just like him.

Others are around, but I don't know who they are. I've been told by a psychic that a man who shows up from time to time, smoking heavily, is a family member. I am supposed to know him, but he never lets me see him. I think it's him making all the noises to get my attention. He's just trying to have some fun. He thinks it's funny and it's not hurting anyone. The vanilla scent is either my grandma or my friend Kitty. I'm not sure of the others' identities.

Daddy's Visit

One quiet night I was in the den at the computer reviewing EVPs when I saw a reflection on the screen of someone walking behind me. But nobody was there.

Another time at the computer, I sensed a man come up behind my left shoulder and lean over to see what I was watching on the monitor. He straightened up and left through the door without saying a word. I just knew it was my dad. I mentally asked, "Why don't you come more often?"

"I'll try," I heard him answer. Then the touch lamp came on.

The next day a white shadow came out of the den and disappeared right before my eyes.

A week went by. Out of the blue, I got the strongest feeling that I was supposed to go somewhere, but I didn't get any indication of where or when. Later that day I was notified that my uncle had passed away. He looked just like my grandfather on my dad's side of the family, except that he had snowy white hair.

I went to the funeral home to pay my respects and was immediately assailed by the overpowering odor of cigarette smoke. All the members of my family who had already passed away, including Daddy, were gathered around the casket and seemed to be having a good old time. They were smoking, having a beer (root beer), laughing, and talking among themselves.

Changes

A lot of changes were taking place on the SPIRITswp team, including changing the team logo, color, and positions. I was just beginning to understand my gift, and these changes were extremely distracting. It was also distracting, when the team was involved in an investigation, for me to get visions of things that had absolutely nothing to do with the case. I just couldn't handle the complications involved. I had too many other things on my mind, so I resigned. It was a great team. I miss it and still keep in touch with many of the members and former members who became friends.

I was recruited by two other teams. One was the Paranormal Research Team, led by John Anthony. I helped out on a few cases.

The other team was the Mon Valley Paranormal Research Team, led by its co-founder, April Roberts. One day I was talking with April about everyday, inconsequential, personal stuff, when a question popped into my consciousness.

I asked if she was working on a certain case. She said yes. So I started filling her in on details about it. I had received crucial information she needed to know. April was flabbergasted to hear what I knew. She asked me if I could help her and her team with the case. I agreed, providing that I would be acting on a consultant basis and that John Anthony was all right with it.

April sent me a photo of a location where her team was conducting an investigation. As soon as I brought it up on my computer screen, I started writing information about the paranormal investigation. It was imperative that April get this information as soon as possible.

April wrote back that what I had been seeing had already happened to her team during the investigation. Then I told her about certain places at the location that the team hadn't yet investigated. There were spirits there, and I told her who the spirits were. She later informed me that my information was spot on. I assisted her with another case as well.

Then a third team that was just forming asked me to join. I politely declined all offers. The third team never materialized. The two teams that were already up and running wouldn't take no for an answer. They asked if I would at least help them out occasionally, as needed, even if I wouldn't be a full-time member. I said okay on one condition. I would act as a consultant for both teams only so long as neither team had any problems with me consulting the other.

We Don't Talk About Those Kinds of Things

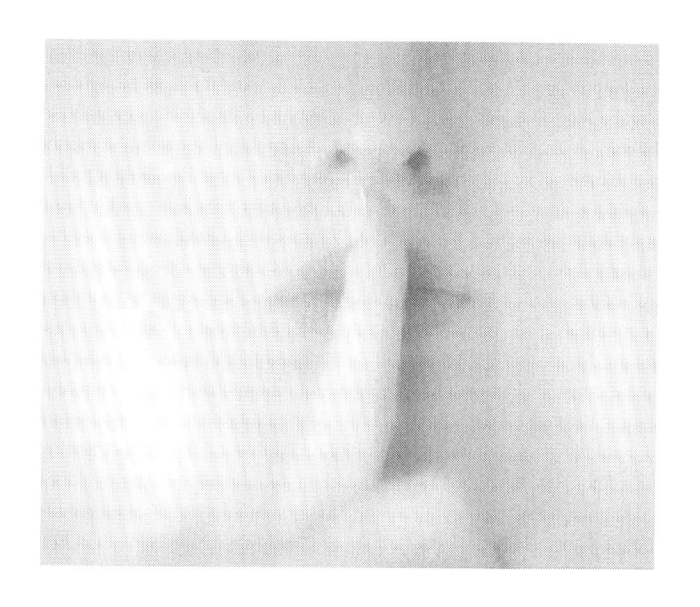

Phase 6: I Am a Psychic

Happenings

Some of the places where investigations take place are just too far away for me to get there. In those cases, the leader of the group sends me a picture of the place they are going to investigate. Often I can pick up a good bit of information about the place from the photo, and I pass that information to the group. It isn't the same as being physically present at the pictured location, but sometimes I make a connection and I feel as though I am there.

When the investigation is completed, the team shares the results, confirming my psychic readings of the photos. Time after time, I've been told that I had furnished more information and more reliable information than the client.

In fact, clients have been surprised to learn that the teams already knew things the clients had forgotten to tell them.

Things went along smoothly. I enjoyed serving as an outside consultant to the teams. One day a member of one team asked if I would join the new team they were starting. I declined that offer and lost contact with that person.

To this day I still maintain friendships with many of the people I met in the paranormal investigative teams. Some are still members of the team I belonged to, some have teams of their own, and others are just keeping in touch. Even though I am no longer on a team, I will be forever grateful to those who helped me discover and develop my abilities, guide me in their use, and once and for all, *not* feel weird.

On a visit to West Overton Museums in Scottdale, Pennsylvania, my family and I took a guided tour of the Overholt Mansion, where 19th-century robber baron (or industrialist, if you prefer) Henry Clay Frick spent his childhood. In one of the bedrooms was an original desk that Overholt family members used during the mid-1800s. Jeremy reached to open a drawer. When I pushed his hand away, my hand touched the desk.

I was instantly transported back to an earlier time in our nation's history. It was the same room, but now there was a man wearing period clothing standing at the desk working. As if I had made an unwanted interruption in his daily routine, he turned his head to the right and locked eyes with me. He stared at me for a while. Then, in the blink of an eye, I found myself back in the present as though nothing had happened. Nobody around me noticed my adventure. That is one of my strangest experiences.

Remember when I went to the psychic for answers and was told that I am sensitive and empathetic? And I thought I didn't get an answer? I was wrong. I just didn't understand the answer. Now I do. When she told me I was sensitive, it was her way of telling me that I was psychic.

She also told me that I was empathetic. An empath can feel exactly what someone else is feeling. The feelings have to be intense to trigger my ability. Of course, like everything else that has come my way from the spirit world, I've learned about this the hard way.

Flight 93

My family and I decided to visit the Flight 93 Memorial in Shanksville, Pennsylvania, where forty heroic Americans lost their lives in the September 11 attacks. When they fought the hijackers to regain control of the plane, it crashed into the countryside at over 500 miles per hour and disintegrated.

We went there to pay our respects to these heroes. Traveling eastward on U.S. Route 30 was a pleasant ride, but as soon as we turned onto the road to the crash site, I felt the change. Tears oozed from my eyes and I had a heavy, foreboding feeling in my heart. We parked in the lot and walked to the dedication area. All my feelings intensified and I became more and more grief-stricken.

We looked out over the huge, empty, rolling field, where a solitary American flag ruffled in the breeze. Someone, maybe a park ranger, told us that the flag marked the exact spot where the plane had crashed into the ground. I could see that – and much, much more.

Pandemonium reigned. People were stumbling around, dazed. Some were crying and screaming for help. A man wearing a red tie and a blue dress shirt with its sleeves rolled to the elbow walked toward the nose of the airplane. He was cradling his left arm as though it was broken.

A dazed-looking woman with brown curly hair held her bleeding right temple. Others milled about screaming for help. People were everywhere. The confusion and hysteria were so overwhelming that I started to shake and cry.

"Bev, Bev, what's the matter? Are you okay?" John asked.

"John, it's horrible. I've never seen anything like this. All these poor people, and there's nothing I can do for them."

He cradled me in those big powerful arms where I have always been able to feel safe and protected.

"Bev, do you want me to take you back to the car? Do you want to leave?"

Before I could answer, I saw a flight attendant waving her arms over her head and shouting out, "Hey! We're over here. Please! We need help!" I can't even remember whether I answered John because those feelings of utter helplessness and heartbreak had become unbearable.

I wished with all my heart that I could do something, anything to help.

"You *can* help. We're over here."

Oh, my God. The flight attendant had heard me!

I turned to John and told him that I was going to try to get these poor people to cross over, if I could. I knew that it was a massive undertaking, more difficult than anything I had ever tried to do before. And more important. If I could just get them to realize that they were dead and no longer belonged on this side, maybe they would cross over. I had no idea whether this would work.

I tried to explain to the flight attendant that the plane had crashed and nobody survived. I must have gotten through to her. She stopped what she was doing and stood there in shock.

"We're all dead?" she said. "I'm dead?" She turned and walked away slowly.

I was shaken out of my train of thought by my son tugging at me, complaining. It was too hot, he was hungry, and he wanted to leave now. I had had about all I could handle and wanted to leave as well. I've never been back.

I had told John that I would like to see the site both before and after the memorial was built, but I'm not sure whether I can ever go back. Maybe someday.

Random Knocks

Back at home, it was SSDD: same stuff, different day. Winter blew in with a fresh snowfall. Mom wasn't home. John, Jeremy, and I were in the living room playing *Deal or No Deal* on TV. Jeremy went back to his room to look for something. While we waited for him to return, John and I talked about my dad.

We were interrupted by three distinct, sharp knocks on the bay window next to where we sat. Outside the bay window was a wooden deck. During the winter we never used that entrance; too much snow piled up against it. We never bothered to clear the deck or the steps leading up to it. Besides, we hadn't heard anyone walking on the deck.

Just to be sure, I got up and turned on the outside light. Nobody was on the deck, and there wasn't a single footprint in the snow that covered it. We came to the conclusion that it was my dad rapping on the window to let us know he was around because we had been talking about him. He would. He had that kind of a sense of humor.

We Don't Talk About Those Kinds of Things

Missing, Maybe Murdered

We made it through the holidays, and winter 2011 was fully upon us. Nothing too bad, though; I'd seen worse. Even so, the gray days were depressing.

One morning early in the year, my mother showed me a newspaper photo of a missing woman and asked if I could help with that particular case. I guess her denial was evaporating. I said that I wasn't sure, but I'd try.

One look at the picture had me transfixed by the missing woman's eyes. I heard her say, "Help me." The article didn't give me much to go on. I didn't want to be late for work, so I stuffed the newspaper in my bag with my lunch.

At lunch I took the newspaper from the bag and once again was held in thrall by her eyes. Again I heard her say, "Help me." I wanted to spend more time with the picture to see if I could learn something, but I had to go back to work.

That night before going to bed, I looked once again into her eyes and asked, "Where could you be?" Then I went to sleep. I'm not sure whether it came to me in a dream or a vision in a state of semi-consciousness, but I saw her hiding behind a tree in a wooded area.

The next day, I ran into a very good friend of mine from the SPIRITswp team. Dennis Overly, a retired private investigator, and I had kept in touch. We were talking about this case and the things I was picking up from the picture. A few days later, I called Denny to describe other things about the case I was picking up. He said he would help me piece them together.

Night after night I would ask for signs that would help locate the woman or tell me how to get to her. Night after night, I got the same visions. I kept trying, and one night I got a few more signs.

I asked Denny for advice on what to do now that I had more information. We decided to work the case together.

I called the police to tell them that I had visions of images that could help them solve the case. Nobody called back. I finally found out that the investigating officer was on vacation, so I left a message and waited. And waited.

After a week, I called again. This time I was told that another officer was on the case now, but when I tried to contact him, I was told he'd be gone until next week. By now I just wanted to give someone the information that I had. I was told that an officer would call me back.

Two hours later the phone rang. It was an officer prepared to take my information. Or at least he said he was. I gave him the information that I had been picking up on. The only real question he asked me was "When you said you saw her, did you witness anything at that time?"

I replied, "No. I'm a psychic and it came to me in the form of a vision."

I could almost hear him saying, "Yeah, right." He took my basic information: name, address, phone number. He told me he would put everything in a folder and place it on the investigating officer's desk. I never heard from anybody in that police department again. I suspect he confused the investigating officer's desktop with the wastebasket.

Attitudes like that are just one of the reasons I'm reluctant to identify myself as a psychic/medium.

Denny said never mind, we would just go ahead and find out what happened on our own. We made a good team. Denny was great with doing research and coming up with ideas. I kept a running log of what I was able to pick up. I kept getting a mental picture of a restaurant and gas station near where she lived.

Every night I asked the question, "Where do I go from here?" I received a mental picture of me standing in front of the restaurant, then turning to the left and looking at a road.

I shared this with John. To his credit, he believed in me enough to suggest that we could go for a ride down that road early Saturday. Meanwhile, I picked up on a blue car and a man's first name. I wasn't sure what the name meant. Was it the name of the driver of the blue car? Was it the name of the assailant? Or was it maybe a place or something appearing on a road sign? I just didn't know.

Long rides never bother us, so it was no hardship to load up bright and early Saturday morning for our trip. We eventually found the gas station and the restaurant within a mile of one another, and I *knew* we had found the right spot. I stood in front of the restaurant, looked to my left, and was convinced that was the proper road to take. It felt as though she was giving me directions.

On faith we followed that road to its end. We had to make a choice: left or right?

The blue car appeared, the one from my vision. The same color, make, and model.

Sounding like a detective in an old TV show, I said, "Follow that car."

John replied, "Okay, but maybe not very far because we need gas."

Imagine our surprise when that blue car pulled into the next gas station. After filling up, we continued to follow it. We were unfamiliar with the road and drove a bit slower than the blue car, so it was soon out of sight. We continued driving.

The area started looking strangely familiar, even though I had never been there in my life. I puzzled over that for a few minutes. After a while, John said that it was getting late and we should head home. The words were no sooner out of his mouth than he pointed out a sign by the road. On it was the name from my vision. We were on the right track! I was sure of it. She was leading me to her. But that day we had to head back home.

I contacted Denny, my investigative partner, and brought him up to date.

The next weekend we headed back, only this time we started at that sign by the road. John pointed the car in the direction we'd headed last week and just drove. I'd tell him what to do when the time came.

A short distance down the road I saw a road off to the side and told John to turn onto it.

"Where are we going and what should I be looking for?" John wanted to know.

"I don't know," I replied. "I'll tell you when I know. I'm being led somewhere, but I don't know where."

"Okay," John said. "But if I hear gunshots, I'm getting us the hell out of here."

He wasn't joking.

Just then I told him to pull over. We got out of the car and I stood still, waiting for directions. Sure enough, I was pulled toward the woods along the road. All the while I kept picturing the tree I had seen her hide behind in my vision. Suddenly I stopped in my tracks. I looked to my right and there it was: the tree she had tried to use for protection.

I tried to communicate with her while standing next to the tree. We were in the area where she wanted us to be. I got an impression of a person walking through the woods near me, a nebulous form I couldn't identify as male or female. The woods were open enough that someone walking there should be easy to see.

It was getting late and we had to head home, so I said goodbye to the woman and told her I would come back. I also took a few pictures before we left.

Once again, I gave Denny a status report. He was

amazed at how my visions brought us to the restaurant and how my vision directed us to the tree, about an hour's drive from the restaurant.

When John had to work the following weekend, Denny went with me. He brought all the paranormal investigative equipment he had, and I brought mine as well. He and I got into the habit of making a weekly trek to the wooded area. We took our K II meters, digital voice recorders, and assorted other equipment.

The first couple of weekends we got some EVPs (Electronic Voice Phenomena). Denny and I would hear a girl's or young woman's voice calling, "Help!"

"Where are you?" we'd ask."We want to help."

"Come up," was the answer.

We didn't always get answers to our questions, but I always knew that she was there. One time, after a particularly frustrating day, Denny and I were leaving. It seemed pointless to put in all this time and effort and have nothing to show for it. We were beginning to wonder if she even wanted us there. He said to the air, "We won't be coming back."

"Wait! Come back," the girl's voice pleaded.

Of course we went back the next weekend.

When John, Jeremy, and I went there, we heard footsteps when none of us were moving.

One time my mother and I went there. We both (yes, both) heard footsteps approaching us from behind. I was pelted by invisible acorns hitting my head. All this activity was enough to convince us that there was an entity in that area.

Another weekend when neither John nor Denny could make the trip, my mother volunteered to drive, and then my sister asked if she and her daughter could come. So five of us jammed into Sis's car for the trip.

When we finally arrived at our destination, the first

thing out of Sis's mouth was "How in the heck did you find this place?"

I just gave her one of my best smiles.

We'd been there only a short time when Mom's camera stopped working. After we tinkered with it for some time, it started functioning again, and Mom took some pictures. However, they all came out almost black. Then it quit again. After the third time this happened, it came back on and started taking good pictures.

Sis's cellphone kept ringing. When she answered it, there was never anybody on the other end. Then it just went dead. Sis went back to the car to try to charge her phone battery. Then my phone died too.

And my K II meter was going off the scale. It not only pegged to the highest reading, red, but it stayed there for more than a minute at a time.

After nearly two hours of spirits' antics, it was time to go home. It was getting late and the kids were getting hungry. Walking toward the car, Sis used the remote control to unlock the car doors. But they didn't unlock. So she waited until we were nearly at the car and tried again. No luck.

She was about to use her key when the car doors spontaneously unlocked on their own. All my equipment was already shut down.

The radio started changing stations all by itself. Sis reset the radio and plugged in her cellphone. It was lit up to the Charley Project, an international lost-children network. She shut off her cellphone and turned it back on again, which seemed to cure the problem.

I decided to turn on the K II as well as the voice recorder. The voice recorder wouldn't cooperate. I asked Sis to lower the car windows and then turn off the engine so the various electrics and electronics in the car wouldn't interfere with what I wanted to do. The K II was giving

We Don't Talk About Those Kinds of Things

readings all the way to the top again, and I tried to use my cellphone as a video recorder. While I was asking questions of the entity, the K II meter went off and the cellphone stopped recording video.

My little niece was getting scared, so I said farewell to the entity and told her I'd be back. We shut everything down. As we drove away, Sis's cellphone went back to the Charley Project.

As soon as we put some distance between us and that wooded area, everything went back to normal.

Wow! While I was surprised at the amount of activity we encountered, I was even more surprised that my mom and my sister wanted to help me figure out what had happened. My sister is a bit fearful of the whole paranormal thing and my mom is the one who always used to say, "We don't talk about those kinds of things."

Denny and I examined microscopically everything that happened on our trips. With the little I've indicated here, along with other information that has come our way, we have an idea of where she is.

Since all we had in the way of evidence were a few EVPs, some digital pictures that varied in quality from good to bad, videos ditto, and K II indicating anomalies in the red zone, we couldn't go to the police yet. Based on all his years of experience as a private investigator, Denny was sure we just didn't have what the police would regard as solid evidence.

We decided to take a break from our investigation and renew it again when we could look at everything with recharged batteries, so to speak.

While Denny did some more research, I went on a much-needed vacation with my family.

Gettysburg

During the summer of 2011, my family and I went to Gettysburg for our vacation. Yes, the most haunted place in America. It was a fun vacation, and I had paranormal experiences every day of it.

On the very first day, while we were exploring the town, one store gave me the heebie-jeebies the instant I walked through the door. The place was full of Civil War memorabilia. Walking deeper into its musty confines, I could feel unworldly eyes staring at me from the second-floor loft. I told John that I didn't feel good about this place and we should leave.

Suddenly my son darted up the stairs. Fearful for both his safety and the safety of anything on display up there, I followed as quickly as I could. All the way up the stairs I felt those eyes staring. Just staring.

Memories flooded over me, and I felt dizzy and nauseated. I had to grab a railing to keep from falling. I fought the feelings that enveloped me.

When I finally made it to the second floor, I encountered the person who was staring so intently at me. He was a soldier in a Civil War uniform of the United States, a billy yank. He stood there nonchalantly with a rifle over his right shoulder, staring at us. I couldn't fathom his intention, but I sensed that he did not bear me goodwill. I had to get to the outside air and the nearest garbage can as quickly as possible. Then we headed back to the car.

The farther from that store I got, the better I felt. By the time we were back at the hotel, I felt only a few lingering effects.

The next day, I was in the lobby, about to return to

our room on the fourth floor. As I approached the elevator, the Up button lit, and the elevator doors opened. There was nobody in sight and nobody exited the elevator.

I entered the elevator, pushed the button for my floor, and murmured, "Thank you" to the person to my right. When I stepped out of the elevator on the fourth floor, I realized that there was nobody physically present with me in that elevator.

I had thanked a spirit who was polite enough to open the door for me. If he was courteous enough to open the door, I was courteous enough to thank him. *Okay*, I thought, *about time I get a little respect from the other side.*

The Soldier with the Cadaverous Eyes

That day we went to a few more stores. One of them had everything, including wall hangings. At the top of the stairs was a wall hanging that featured old sepia photos of the faces of four men. I gave the pictures a passing glance, but I was stopped dead in my tracks, frozen with fear at the sight of one of them. I was transported back to my grandmother's house and the Confederate cavalry officer.

I will never forget that face. That red hair and scruffy beard. But most of all those black eyes just staring malevolently at a young girl. And the laughing. The door he held shut just long enough to terrify her. I now know who it was. I was face to face with Lieutenant General James Longstreet of the Army of Virginia.

Research says that Longstreet never set foot in Mount Pleasant, Pennsylvania, but who's to say he didn't pay a little incognito visit there sometime during his life?

I know for sure that he visited that little town after his death and stayed there for years.

What I saw in that store left me feeling uncomfortable for the rest of the day, but that didn't stop me from having fun. We took a tour of the battlefield and I had no distractions other than the occasional soldier walking by who wasn't a re-enactor.

My biggest problem that day had nothing to do with the supernatural. It was the five-story lookout tower. Of course Jeremy, who was fourteen years old now, could move fast and wanted to scamper to the top to find out how far he could see from that height. Height, that nasty word. John and I are both less than comfortable when our feet aren't firmly planted on the ground. And the farther from the ground our feet get, the more uncomfortable we get.

Jeremy ran to the top while John and I reluctantly crawled up the steps. As soon as I got to the top, I found the seats in the middle, as far from the railings as a person can get. I firmly planted my posterior on that bench to catch my breath, and not just from the five-story climb. John did likewise.

Jeremy leaned over the railing, laughing at how small the cars in the lot looked. Eventually I gathered enough courage to go toward the railing, but I suddenly realized just how high up we were and backed away. I would have liked to grab Jeremy and pull him back from the railing.

Instead, I called out that it was time to go. John was as relieved as I was. I edged my way to the stairs and carefully started down one step at a time. I'd never moved so slowly in my life. As I got closer to the ground, my speed picked up until I don't think that even Jeremy could have caught me. That solid ground was like a magnet. At least I can now say, "Been there—-done that. And I won't ever do it again." John completely agrees with me.

After the battlefield tour, we visited the Jennie Wade House. That was a sad place for me because I could see bits

We Don't Talk About Those Kinds of Things

and pieces of what happened on that fateful day 150 years ago. In the basement, where Jennie's body was taken after she was shot, a bed against the wall was roped off with a chain. Neither John nor I was close to the chain or the bed. Jeremy was looking at pictures in another room. Suddenly, on its own, the chain started to swing to and fro.

One of the tour guides had said, "If you're one of the lucky ones, you will see that chain move on its own. We like to think it's Jennie Wade letting us know that she's still here."

After this stroke of "luck," we decided it was a good time to go out for a bite to eat.

That evening we went for a walk along the street where all the ghost tours are located. We hoped to follow one of the tours on our own just to see the sights and places of interest along the way. As we stopped and read the signs about the tours, we were invited to sign up for a ghost tour of one of the houses thought to be haunted.

"No, thank you," John told the agent.

"But we'll teach you all about the equipment we use to investigate the paranormal. You'll be able to tell all your friends that you've been on an actual paranormal investigation."

I looked at John and he looked at me. We both laughed.

"I've already been on many investigations with my own equipment," I informed him.

"Great!" he replied. "You can use your own equipment to investigate this house."

"Not tonight."

We continued on our evening walk. John laughed when I said I could probably tell that guy a thing or two.

The next day we were scheduled to leave. I woke up so dizzy and nauseated that I didn't know how I would be able to travel all the way home. I remembered waking up in the middle of the night knowing there was someone else in the room.

Then I saw him: a soldier standing there watching me. He had followed me back to the hotel room from the antique store. I have no idea what he wanted, since he wouldn't respond to my questions. He did take a step back when I told him he was too close to me and was making me sick.

But it was too late. I came fully awake, already sick to my stomach. At least it wasn't Lieutenant General Longstreet. Being too close to the bogeyman of my childhood probably would have made me deathly ill.

In the morning, after John and Jeremy left the room, I attempted to communicate with the soldier. I told him that my family and I were going home.

"You cannot follow us," I implored him. "You have to stay here."

He didn't answer.

I didn't say anything to John and Jeremy, figuring that I would feel better once we got away. After 100 miles or so, I did feel better.

Renewing the Search

It was a good vacation. I felt recharged. Now it was time to return to work and pick up our daily routines.

Denny and I talked things over a few times and decided to go back to the wooded area in a few weeks. We needed a break from the case of the missing young woman. Some really lousy weather helped us with that decision. A few weeks later the weather cooperated, and we tried to look at everything from a different perspective.

We realized that we *still* had nothing but circumstantial evidence, nothing concrete nor physical that

We Don't Talk About Those Kinds of Things

we could take to the authorities and hand to them.

We tried to rattle the girl a couple of times by telling her that we weren't coming back. We said that it wasn't worth our time when we weren't getting anything in return.

I tried to explain to her that we needed something tangible that we could take to the police. Some kind of physical evidence that they could see and touch. Just a trinket, a piece of jewelry, or a scrap of cloth would do. Anything she had with her when she disappeared. Besides, winter was approaching and it just wouldn't be possible to make these long trips. She didn't respond.

Denny and I agreed to make one last trip that season, but I kept getting a really bad feeling about staying there that day. From past experience we knew that my feelings are usually dead-on (bad choice of words), so we left.

A few days later, I experienced a disturbing premonition in the form of a dream. I called Denny and told him that it was a good thing we were done with that particular investigation for the year. My premonition was of a man approaching us in the woods with a shotgun.

So there would be no more personal visits that year. We would confine ourselves to doing research for the time being.

The first two months of 2012 found me on medical leave from work. Nothing much in the way of paranormal activity was happening.

Denny and I talked about resuming our investigation, but I told him that it was just too dangerous right then. I felt extreme danger for both of us if we went back. We still haven't gone back to this day.

That's not to say that we don't discuss it often. It is, after all, still an unsolved case, and we still have our teeth sunk into it like a pair of piranhas on a fresh kill (another bad choice of words.)

Another Murder

In the meantime, I've been asked to help out with another case. The authorities have decided to reopen it to determine whether it was murder or suicide. I know it wasn't suicide.

Finally, an Un-Haunted House ... so far

The year 2012 brought a new beginning for our little family. John and I bought a house! Though it's 85 years old, it's new to us. We've started making changes that will make it fit us like a glove. So far, nothing unusual (if you know what I mean) has been happening. Mom put the trailer up for sale and moved in with Sis.

A Visit with a Matriarch and a Servant, Both Long Gone

At Christmastime 2012, Mom, Sis, and I, along with my niece and my son, decided to enjoy Mount Pleasant's Festival of Lights at the historic Samuel Warden Mansion. Each year this event is an important fundraiser for the local chapter of the Daughters of the American Revolution. The DAR has owned the building since 1960, so naturally the mansion is known locally as the DAR house. It is annually decorated with dozens of Christmas trees. It's also haunted by the spirit of one of the original owners, Margaret Warden, and one of her servants, a teenage girl named Rebekah.

It was a chilly and overcast November night when we arrived, perfect mood-setting weather for visiting a haunted house.

We Don't Talk About Those Kinds of Things

On the other hand, all the bright holiday lights and festive decorations made this the unlikeliest of places to harbor grim spirits. And so it is. The spirits of the DAR house are playful and benign. They seem happy with their lot in the afterlife.

Once inside the sedate Victorian three-story squarish brick building, we were enveloped in nineteenth-century festivity. There was so much to see that we didn't know which way to go. Our minds were made up for us when the kids dashed off to see the trees in the room to the right.

After exploring all the first floor had to offer and promising the kids some hot chocolate on the way out, we headed for the second-floor displays. We went by way of the main staircase, which immediately brought back memories of my grandparents' house and the experiences I'd had there. I didn't want to cast a shadow on our evening, so I didn't say anything. Nobody else would understand, anyway.

Halfway up the staircase was a small landing equipped with two period chairs and a small stand with a lamp, overlooked by a frosted window. The chairs looked so inviting that, without even thinking about it, I sat down. I was instantly transported to the 1890s. I became a member of the Warden family, even dressed in clothing of that period and class. I looked through eyes that existed nearly 125 years ago. I was jolted out of my experience when the kids called to me from the top of the stairs.

Climbing the staircase to the second floor, I looked up to see exactly which room the kids were calling me from. When I did, I made eye contact with Mrs. Margaret Warden herself. She was standing outside her bedroom wearing a pale blue dress covered with a white wrap, just as she must have done when she was alive all those years ago.

She gazed at me with a peaceful, pleasant smile of welcome, as though she was happy to show off her home all decorated for the season. I looked down just for a second to be sure of my footing on the old steps. When I looked up again, she had disappeared.

Entering that room at the top of the staircase, I found Mom, Sis, and the kids all marveling at the Christmas trees there. One at the bottom of the bed caught my attention. It was decorated with stringed popcorn and paper chains, just as it would have been during the era when the house was at its greatest. It looked perfectly at home. While I didn't see Margaret in that room, I did feel an unmistakable female presence.

The rest of the second floor was heavily decorated with trees and gift baskets, each with some sort of a theme. The themes included baby baskets, toy baskets, game night, movie night, quilting, candy, Steelers, and more others than I can remember. They were all for sale. After all, this was a fundraiser.

The exit route back downstairs was by way of the servants' stairs. On the way to those stairs, I noticed a door to the right that had the sign "Closed to the Public." That door led to the servants' quarters on the third floor. As I gazed at it, the door seemed to become transparent and I could see a young girl in a black dress and white apron sitting on the stairs behind the door.

I said, "Hi, Rebekah."

She looked at me and smiled. Then she stood up and walked toward me. She walked right through the door toward me, but she disappeared at the last minute as though she remembered that she wasn't supposed to interact too much with the living. Rebekah can be a bit of a tease at times, but she is never malicious.

I went back to the first floor for a cookie and something to wash it down. When I realized that I had forgotten to get pictures of the Christmas trees, I headed back upstairs to take some. Mom followed along to keep me company and to take some photos of her own. On the way upstairs, I sat on the other chair on the landing to wait for Mom. This time I felt nothing.

When Mom got to the landing, she said she felt as though something was exerting pressure on her, just shy of enough to make her lose her balance.

"Someone doesn't want me taking pictures," she said jokingly. Was Mom starting to accept presences? Or was she just being a wise acre?

I replied, "I think it was Rebekah saying, 'I'm here.' She's not being mean, just wants noticed."

Mom replied, "Uh huh." She didn't sound convinced.

While Mom was roaming around the second floor taking pictures, I went into Margaret's room. No one else was there just then—except for Margaret, who was lying on her bed smiling and enjoying all the Christmas lights and trees. Then, as other people approached her room, she faded from sight.

Just as we were making ready to leave and Mom was conversing with one of the ladies of the DAR, I felt a spirit come close, so close that I felt a bit nauseated and disoriented. I don't know who or what the spirit was. Neither Margaret or Rebekah would affect me like that.

Even so, I would have liked to stay longer and visit some more with that pair of ladies from the late 1800s. Margaret has a peaceful, calming effect, and Rebekah is a loyal, respectful member of the household staff.

Sometimes Rebekah doesn't approve of the way knick-knacks and other small things are arranged, maybe because that's not how she was taught to arrange them when she was alive. When she thinks things are not in their proper order, she rearranges them.

If you are ever in Mount Pleasant, Pennsylvania, take a ride by the Samuel Warden mansion at 200 Church Street. You just might be one of the fortunate people who look through the windows and see Margaret or Rebekah moving about inside the house.

Some Visions Are Just Too Damn Real!

The sun had long since set, there was a chill in the air, and I had to pick up my hubby from work. Sometimes it's a real inconvenience being a one-car family in a two-car world. It was 9:50 p.m. I told Jeremy that I was leaving to pick up John and to make sure that he had his phone handy just in case.

Leaving the house, I made sure that the porch light was on and the front door was locked behind me. Any parent knows why – just in case.

That chill in the air wasn't just from the weather. Walking toward the car, I got that eerie feeling that someone or something was watching me. I could feel the stare on the back of my head, and it made that space between my shoulder blades tingle.

I swiveled my gaze from side to side. I couldn't see anybody. I couldn't press that button on the remote entry any harder. My thumb ached with the effort and my mind raced, urging that darned door to open faster.

Reaching for the door handle, I turned to the right and got the distinct impression that someone was approaching me. But there was no one there. Just the flash of a black shadow closing on me. I dived into the car and locked all the doors, then double-checked to make sure they were, in fact, locked. I checked the interior of the car and looked out all the windows. There was nobody around.

As I placed the key in the ignition, I froze in place. I couldn't move. I was paralyzed and engulfed in wave upon increasing wave of panic. Suddenly I realized that, despite all

We Don't Talk About Those Kinds of Things

my precautions, I was not alone.

There was a man in the back seat dressed all in black, including a black ski mask. His only concession to color lay in the royal blue gloves on his hands. Those, and the silvery garrote wire extending from one hand to the other. He was going to strangle me!

As the wire came down over my head, passing my face and encircling my neck, I had only one thought: escape. *Move, Bev! You've got to move, Bev,* I thought. *Move or die!*

Somehow sensation returned to my left hand. I found the door handle and wrenched it with all my might, falling out of the car in the process. The open door kept the dome light on, illuminating the car's interior, which was completely empty of humans and other creatures.

There was nobody inside the car. Likewise, there was nobody outside the car--except me. And that feeling of being watched by something unseen.

What in the name of Heaven had just happened to me? I checked again to make sure the car was empty and quickly got back in, and locked the doors. Then I turned on the interior lights and checked again. There was no physical being inside or outside the car, at least as far as I could see.

Thank God I'm safe, I thought, at least temporarily. I tried to gather my wits about me and decipher what had just happened. But I couldn't. Nothing like this had ever happened before or since.

It was then 10:00 p.m. John was done at work, ready to come home. He would be waiting for me wondering why I was late. It's not like me to be late. Even though John's workplace was only a 10-minute drive away, I had to have human contact. I called Jeremy on the phone and talked to him for the entire drive.

When I picked John up, I told him the entire story. Pretty much as I expected, he was noncommittal. And when we got home, he went to bed and fell promptly asleep while I

lay awake for hours. Sometimes men can be so frustrating!
To this day, once the sun sinks below the horizon, I will not set foot outside my house alone.

We Don't Talk About Those Kinds of Things

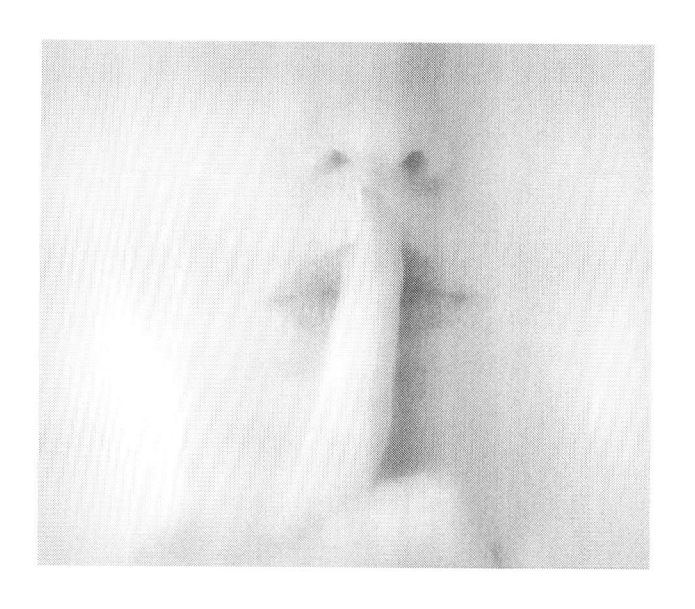

Phase Seven – Investigations

How Paranormal Investigations Are Conducted

First off, remember one thing – our clients' confidentiality is the most important part of any paranormal investigation. Unless clients specifically waive their right to confidential treatment of their information, we closely guard all identifiable details about them as secrets.

There's more than one reason for this. First and foremost, it protects them and their family from misguided ridicule by those who consider everything about the world of paranormal investigation unscientific at best, and bogus at worst. If you have read this far in this book, then you know that I am no stranger to disbelief, criticism, and ridicule, and I have no intention of exposing others to it. So I have disguised our clients' locations and names to the best of my ability in the descriptions of cases in this book.

We Don't Talk About Those Kinds of Things

Let's get started with a hypothetical case to see how paranormal investigations are started.

Someone in the team, usually the team leader, is contacted by someone who requests help with unusual circumstances or happenings in their home or business. If the request isn't first received by the team leader, it is passed on to him or her for vetting.

The leader gathers as much general information about the case as possible, then presents it at one of the regularly scheduled meetings.

Our group had two psychic/mediums, but I am only going to describe only my involvement. As a psychic/medium, I prefer to enter the investigation with a minimal amount of information so that any impressions I receive aren't tainted by preconceived notions. Therefore, I am excluded from preliminary interviews with the clients. That's where the rest of the team comes in.

The preliminary investigation is conducted to determine whether or not the case has enough substantial elements to take it further. This is done by the team leader through interviews with the client and anyone else involved in the incident.

There is paperwork to complete giving us permission to enter the property and investigate.

As soon as that is done, the team enters the property and starts going from room to room checking for temperature changes, EMF spikes, and anything that, in their experience, is out of the ordinary. All of this is dutifully recorded for later analysis. This gives us a baseline for comparison with future investigations.

All investigations start in this manner in order to conform to scientific principles of experimental repeatability.

While there are similarities, personalities are involved, and spirits have as many differing personalities as living entities. Therefore, from this point on, each investigation is unique to the circumstances experienced and reported by the client.

One of My First Investigations

The following is a report of an actual paranormal investigation conducted by SPIRITswp, described from my point of view.

The client's report had been completed by Barry and another member of the team. I was kept in the dark, so to speak, about any particulars outside my own sphere of interaction with the location.

We arrived at the two-story red brick house in a small town, the kind of home and town evoked by the name Mayberry. It sat quietly on a side street sporting a nicely groomed front yard that said,"Welcome." Barry spoke with the client to see if anything new had happened since their last conversation.

While he was doing this, I set up an area of psychic protection around myself and the rest of the team of six. The team spent this time gathering the equipment necessary to get the baseline readings.

I equipped myself with an audio recorder and a K II meter, even though I have difficulty reading the meter while communicating with spirits. Barry returned and we started.

Entering the home, we commenced an intensive walk-through. Barry carried a digital audio recorder and a K II meter while I opened my consciousness to any spirit that might be in the area.

As soon as we entered through the side door, we made the usual audible statements on our recorder for documentation purposes. The statements included our names, the date and time, and our precise location. Immediately after doing this, I constantly scanned the area using all of my senses for any anomalies.

As soon as I was able to psychically sense anything, I attempted to make contact by speaking with any entities in the area and absorbing any emotional energy they emanated.

Then I vocalized my findings for the recorder. Barry and I asked questions constantly. Some examples: "Is there anyone here who would like to talk with us?' "What is your name?" "How many people are here with us?" And of course, we paused and listened for answers.

I had no sooner entered one of the first floor rooms than I spotted a male figure lounging in the corner. Barry, however, was unable to see or sense the figure. The male presence then walked to the next room to the bottom of a flight of stairs with the two of us following, me leading the way.

I asked Barry, "Are we permitted to go upstairs?"

"Sure. Follow me," came the answer. Only it wasn't Barry, it was the spirit talking.

Since he didn't hear it, I relayed the permission to Barry. I followed the spirit about the house, with Barry following closely in our path.

Following the spirit was unusual for me. It wasn't so much a physical imperative as it was an emotional and psychic tugging of my psyche that made me go in a particular direction. I still had my own free will and motor control. I could freely stop to talk with the spirit and with Barry whenever the mood struck me.

The first place we were led was the second floor. At the top of the stairs we were confronted with an open landing that had a wall of closets with mirrors as doors.

Over to the right lay two bedrooms, and to the left a bedroom and a bathroom.

My spirit guide led me to the back bedroom, where he stood looking out the window as though watching for someone or something. He then retraced his steps back across the landing with all the mirrors and entered the bathroom.

More mirrors, this time a half-wall of them. All these mirrors were creeping me out.

Even so, I was drawn to them, almost forced to gaze into them. When I did, I saw my reflection, Barry's reflection off to one side behind me, and a third person. It wasn't the spirit who guided us here; he had disappeared. It was another spirit I can only describe as a dirty man. Not dirty in the sense of unwashed, but rather in the sense of unclean. Unclean as in dirty-minded. This entity likes hanging out in the bathroom and the bedrooms, especially the bathroom. He likes watching the women of the household getting ready in the morning. He showed me how he watches them. Enough said. You get the idea.

By now I was really creeped out. I liked neither the pervert spirit nor all the mirrors. Mirrors are said to be dimensional doorways that allow spirits free access between planes of existence. I'm telling you what they are "said" to be, but I've never heard it actually proved with empirical evidence. Nevertheless, I was more than happy to leave both them and the second floor behind.

Our earlier ghostly guide returned when we reached to the bottom of the stairs and I bombarded him with questions, as did Barry. Though he was not being difficult, he answered our questions only when the mood struck him.

Eventually we found ourselves in the basement standing at a door that led to the outside. At least that's what the door appeared to be to Barry. I wasn't so sure.

I stopped before I got too close to that door just because I couldn't go any farther, it was too crowded. I told Barry a large number of people were passing through that door as we approached it. So many, in fact, that I had to press my back up against the wall so that I wouldn't block them.

As they passed, I felt a chill, something like you get when you open a freezer door and the cold rolls out.

One that I remember in particular was a lady dressed in Victorian attire, complete with one of those big flowery hats. As she walked by me, she gave me a knowing look, acknowledging my presence. Then she promptly disappeared into nothingness.

This wasn't just a doorway, it was a portal between the spirit and the physical world, allowing the spirits to pass from one plane to another. I thought I heard the number one hundred or more, but I'm not sure.

Continuing through the basement allowed me to regain my equilibrium. I had gotten a bit lightheaded and dizzy, but it quickly passed. The vortex located at that doorway had caused my vertigo, and the farther I got from it the more I recovered.

We wound our way up to the first floor again and entered the kitchen. There I saw a black shadow flitting through that room. It was another male spirit, a different one from the first. He passed so quickly that I nearly missed him altogether. I was finished for the day, both physically and psychically.

Barry and I left the house and stayed with the clients outside while the rest of the team went inside to get baseline readings and scout for appropriate places to set up the investigative equipment.

A time and date was set for the in-depth investigation. The size and complexity of the site determined that all team members would be needed, but I would not be able to make it.

For the investigation all necessary equipment and supplies were checked, rechecked, and packed. Extra, fully charged batteries are always necessary because spirits use energy to manifest themselves and batteries are frequently the closest source of that energy. It is common for batteries to drain during the course of an investigation.

Atmospheric and lunar data was collected and recorded. Weather data was also collected, with special attention to possible storm cycles. That's because all the excess energy provided by storms makes it easier for spirits to communicate.

Then after the investigation was completed, all of the team equipment was turned in and all the audio data from all the recorders was downloaded for examination and evaluation.

There were hours and hours of audio data, and we all had to listen to it for evidence.

I learned that I had a knack for audio evaluation and enjoyed finding those places where spirits communicated with us. For instance, that male spirit who said, "Sure, follow me," had his statement captured on audio.

Many answers to my questions were also captured, including answers that I couldn't hear at the time they were given because of the tremendous amount of energy it takes for a spirit to be physically audible. It is much less draining for them to answer via digital recorder.

I was amazed at how much audible evidence I was able to gather and how readily my questions were answered by the spirits. Since I have always been unsure of both myself and my abilities, this validated me as a psychic in a way that nothing else could.

There was actually two-way communication between me and the spirit world.

Once all the evidence was collected, collated, and evaluated, it was presented to the client. This is called the reveal. I was not able to go to this particular reveal, so the case was closed as far as I was concerned.

My Last Investigation with SPIRITswp

I loved my time with SPIRITswp. The group, especially Barry, helped me nurture and develop my abilities without being judgmental or impatient.

As my time progressed with SPIRITswp, I was eventually given the responsibility of being the administrator of the public forum. Although it sounds a bit grandiose, the position is basically a monitoring one. It was my job to communicate with the public, answer their questions, and foster their interest in the paranormal sciences.

We also got cases to investigate through the public forum. People contact the group's website to ask questions, ask for help, and tell us things about hauntings, UFO sightings, Bigfoot appearances and so on. It is the administrator's job to handle these questions and comments and, when called for, refer them to Barry.

One day while monitoring the traffic on the public forum, I noticed someone's questions about paranormal investigations and their inner workings.

While answering her questions about how long investigations take and how soon they can be scheduled, I realized that she was actually trying to ask us to do an investigation. For obvious reasons I didn't want her to give any information on a public forum that could identify her or her location, so I gave her my personal email address within the team. I explained to her that that way she could ask questions of a more personal nature without violating her confidentiality.

After a few emails had crossed the Internet between us, she asked how soon we could start and how long it would take to resolve her problem.

At that point I stepped out and turned the case over to Barry, not just because he's the team leader but also because as a psychic/medium on the team, I don't want to have more than the barest minimum of information about any case I may be called on to work.

I personally need to go into a case cold, gathering information only through my senses and abilities without any outside influences or information. This keeps me objective and validates my abilities.

To this day, I still wallow in self-doubt and need that enforcement that finding things through my own psychic ability brings. It is a constant learning experience, both in how to use my abilities and how to develop them.

So I referred the potential client to Barry, but not before I gave him a heads up about a vibe I was getting. I was receiving the word "DANGER" in big, bold, black letters. Due to that and other impressions I received, I told him that he should take this case seriously. Barry assigned one of the other team members to collect the preliminary information from the possible client.

At the next meeting of the team, Barry announced that the session would be shortened that evening because he was meeting some new clients that night. Later, when the client and her family arrived, once again I picked up on the word "DANGER" and received a general feeling of malice.

I felt my gaze being inexorably drawn to them time after time. Barry noticed this and asked me to step outside with him. Once we were alone, he asked me, "Bev, are you getting something new about this case?"

"Only the renewed indication of danger," I answered
"Have you talked with anybody about this?"

"No."

I gave him what I thought was the real name of the client, who had used a pseudonym in her earlier communications with me on the public forum.

Barry confirmed that I did indeed have the name right. He and another member of the team interviewed the family, got the specifics of the case, and set up an appointment for the walk-through.

When we arrived, Barry talked with the clients as they were getting ready to leave so we could conduct the investigation. I sensed that someone was going to be ill in the near future. This was a shock to me; I had never gotten a premonition of illness. I wasn't sure what to make of it, so I didn't mention it until I could think it over. It was out of the blue, and I wasn't sure if it was right or not.

Then, as the client and her family walked past me, I got the definite impression that it was she who would be ill, the next time I saw her. But the feeling was tentative enough that I put it out of my mind to concentrate on the matter at hand.

As always, before entering an area where paranormal activity is suspected, I set up an aura of protection around myself and the other investigators who would be entering. This is actually less imposing than it sounds. What I do is envision an area of white light around us. Then I say a little prayer, and we are all set.

Barry and I walked into the house, turning on the K II meter and the voice recorder once we were there. We stated our names, the date and time, the location, and our reasons for being there.

Once that little bit of necessary documentation was out of the way, he said, "Hello. We are here to talk with whoever is here with us tonight."

He went on, "We are not here to harm you in any way or to disrespect you."

The SPIRITswp Team is respectful of the spirits. After all, spirits were just like you and me at one time. They deserve the same treatment that living people do.

Then it was my turn to say, "We just want to talk with you and see you. I am able to see you, even if my friend Barry can't. The equipment you see here with us will help those who cannot see or hear you. It will not harm you in any way."

You see, a lot of the equipment we use today hasn't been around for very long, and the spirits may have never seen anything like it. Just like living beings, they can be afraid of the unknown. And just like living beings, when they are fearing something, they will try to hide from it. Which makes it difficult, if not impossible, to communicate with them. So to allay their fears, we explain each piece of equipment we use and its purpose.

Then I reach out psychically and head in whatever direction I am drawn. I go from place to place, area to area, and room to room, to see what I can pick up. I keep up a running commentary about what I am hearing, seeing, and feeling as I go. On that particular investigation I asked, "Please, give me a sign that you are here."

We eventually wended our way through the house to the attic, where I saw an older man. I felt that he moves about quite a bit in that attic. He considers it his ideal hiding spot. I couldn't learn who or what he was hiding from. I did learn that he enjoys looking out the attic window to see who is coming and going.

Then I felt a tugging at my consciousness that drew me downstairs to the first floor.

"I hear doors banging," I told Barry. "Cupboard doors, and maybe the front and rear exterior doors too."

When we reached the front door, I placed my hand flat on the inside of it to get an impression. I got a communication from another spirit, another male. He wanted us to go out the door. So we did.

As soon as Barry and I set foot on the porch, I could hear the spirit laughing. He didn't want us to stay in the house and thought it was funny how he tricked us into leaving.

"Yes, well, I don't think you're very funny, and we aren't going to leave," I said. We went back into the house.

Slightly chagrined, the entity led us back to the basement. While there, Barry and I heard footsteps above us on the first floor. He got on the radio and asked the other members of the team if anyone was in the house besides us. When everyone had checked in we realized that we were the only ones in the house, so we raced upstairs to catch whoever was walking around on the first floor. There was nobody. But when we returned to the basement, the walking commenced again.

That male spirit was playing with us, enjoying himself at our expense.

While down there we came across a hole in the floor and I got an immediate mental picture of a gun. It was clear, but at the same time, I couldn't determine whether it had anything to do with the case we were investigating. I felt that I was through for the day and told Barry as much. He decided to bring in the other investigators to see what they could find.

When we arrived at the bottom of the basement stairs, I saw a transparent lady coming down the stairs. Right before she got to the bottom, she disappeared into nothingness. Then I had a quick spell of dizziness. The whole episode happened so quickly that I wasn't sure it had happened at all.

That nailed it – the investigation was over for me.

The other investigators then entered the building to gather what evidence they could. Then Barry called the client back to the house to tell her we were finished for the time being. Imagine my shock when she returned feeling very ill.

My premonition was right on target. I felt a sense of awe at how strong my abilities were getting.

But there is a definite downside to that strength. It requires tremendous energy to maintain. I was completely drained, physically and emotionally. We packed all our gear. By the time I arrived home, I would have liked to go straight to bed. But before I could slip between the sheets for some much-needed rest, I had to record everything I could on paper so that it wouldn't fade from my memory.

We all turned in our reports. They were evaluated and reviewed to glean the best evidence from them, and a reveal was formulated for the client. Then Barry and some other members of the team made an appointment with the client and revealed our findings.

This was my final case with SPIRITswp.

I Go to a Party That Happened 140 Years Ago

One day I got a call from John Anthony of the Paranormal Research Team asking me for help on one of his cases. It sounded interesting, so of course I said yes. When we arrived at the location, I saw a large two-story building with a well-kept, pleasing entrance. Inside was a stairway to the right extending up to the second floor. At the base of the stairway was what seemed to have been a ticket booth at one time, but it was all boarded up now.

Nevertheless, a kindly older gentleman was selling tickets and charming me with his great smile. I was going to comment on his clothing from a bygone era, but it would have been a waste of time. I was the only one who could see him. He seemed to be both happy with his job and in on the joke that only I could see him because he gave me his brightest smile, verging on a laugh.

I looked to my left and saw an antique baby grand piano that looked as though it was made of mahogany.

Straight ahead was a huge ballroom that drew me in. As I was walking to the center of the room, I noticed a small bar over on the left wall. A raised stage was directly in front of me at the other end of the cavernous room. I stopped in the center of the ballroom and pirouetted, taking in the overhanging balcony that ran the length of both sides of the room.

I imagined all the parties, receptions, and conventions that must've taken place there over the years.

While looking up at the balcony, even though I couldn't see anyone, I could feel their eyes on us. I had to go up there, so John and I went back to the foyer and took the stairs to the second floor. As I started up the steps, I turned and waved at the old fellow in the ticket booth. He just kept smiling.

As we climbed the stairs, an elegantly dressed lady circa 1870 descended the same stairway. She smiled hello as she passed us.

At the top of the stairway we walked through an ornate set of double doors and out onto the balcony. Seeing the place as it looked during the late 1800s, I was awestruck with its grandeur. The balcony was wide enough to accommodate tables and chairs, and I could imagine all the people in their finery socializing while waiters flitted about with drinks and hors d'oeuvre.

Enough imagining. I walked along the right side of the balcony and immediately saw an older couple from a bygone era.

I told John that it would be a good idea to set up some cameras on the balcony as well as down in the ballroom proper.

While he was busy with that, I fired up our digital

voice recorder and started talking with that couple while they were still there. I didn't want to miss anything they had to say while the rest of the team was setting up. I politely asked if they would please stay for a few minutes and started asking them some questions. Unfortunately, I got no response. They pretty much ignored me as they walked about enjoying themselves at a party that I could neither see nor get an invitation to join.

I continued to the far end of the balcony and found another stairway. This one led down to the kitchen, and we decided not to go there for the time being.

Turning away, I saw a black shadow traverse the bottom of the stairs. I tried to identify the entity, but to no avail.

John and I continued along the perimeter of the ballroom on the balcony and returned to the entrance way so we could walk the opposite side. Then things got weird. I could walk only so far along that side of the balcony. Something prevented me from walking any farther than halfway back along that side. I tried to move forward, but couldn't. My body just wouldn't obey me. It was like walking into a wall of marshmallows.

I asked John to walk past me, and he had no problem walking all the way to the far end of the balcony. But for me, even backing up was difficult. I tried to fool whatever was preventing my movement by acting as though I was leaving in the opposite direction, then turning and hurrying back, but it didn't work. As soon as I reached that halfway point, I couldn't proceed. I was frozen in place.

I spotted another team member and asked him to go on ahead, but he also was stopped in his tracks. I finally got out of there by retracing my steps back the way I had come. Later on I tried again but was again stopped cold. I couldn't come up with a rational explanation. I guess I just wasn't meant to walk the length of that balcony that night.

Back down on the first floor I noticed that the bartender enjoyed serving drinks, but I had a hard time getting through to him. He kept fading in and fading out. I asked some questions and got some noise on the recorder, but we decided later that it was just equipment noise.

I wasn't picking up anything, so I headed back upstairs with one of the other team members in tow. The old fellow in the ticket booth was gone now, but the lady who had earlier come down the stairs was back at the top again. This time she was pushing away the interior heat with a fan that she was slowly waving back and forth in front of her face. I nodded in her direction and entered the balcony once more, again heading to the right.

It was as though I was being pulled in that direction.

The older couple was still there. Now *they* were watching *me*. Since I had their attention, I asked them how many people were there with us. Their answer was captured on the digital voice recorder as an EVP. They replied, "Ten." When I asked them what year it was, they only laughed. That showed up as an EVP as well.

"Why are you still here?" I asked.

"Because this is our home. We live here," he replied.

I got the impression that the party was being held in their honor, they were having so much fun. Then we heard a faint swell of music as the elderly pair, so deeply in love, walked arm in arm along the balcony and faded from sight.

It was so nice to witness all the people of that time long gone dancing, laughing, and sharing a good time.

That was pretty much it for that night. We packed up, said our good-byes, and went home to examine our evidence and write reports.

Since the place was such a long drive for me, I didn't go to the reveal.

Spooked by a Snake!

After a bit of time passed, John called me again and asked if I would be interested in doing another investigation with him. I asked where it was and, when he told me, I said it was farther than I really wanted to drive. He asked me if there was any way I could help and I told him that if he'd send me a picture of the place in question, I might be able to get something from it. He did, but all I could pick up from the picture was that there was definitely paranormal activity at the place.

I needed to be physically there to get anything more definitive. So even though I really didn't want to, I had to make the drive.

As is my habit, I arrived a few minutes early for the walk-through, but I couldn't get out of my car. There was a snake right smack dab in front of my car crossing the road. And not just any snake, mind you. Ohh, nooo – it was a monster snake that looked like it had escaped from a zoo.

Did I mention that I HATE snakes? Well, just in case I didn't, let me say it right here: I HATE SNAKES! Actually, they petrify me. So you can see that there was no way I was getting out of my car while that monster was out there. I wondered why it hadn't gotten run over, being in the middle of the road and all.

Eventually John showed up, pulled his car next to mine, and asked me what was happening. I told him in no uncertain terms that there was no way on this green earth that I was getting out of my car or going into that building while that snake was on the loose.

He that the snake was probably the owner's pet, and I said I wasn't going into that building unless that beast was locked up somewhere else. John laughed at my reaction. He said that he would go look for the owner.

In no time, the owner came out of the building, held up traffic for a moment, went over and picked up the snake as if it was nothing, and carried it into the building. I stayed safe and sound in my car until John came out and told me that the serpent was locked up in the owner's bedroom and couldn't escape. Only then did I get out of my car and enter the building.

The building was an inn built in the 1700s. John and I entered through the front door and walked through to the back of the building. I checked the kitchen as well as the basement and didn't feel much of anything. I entered one of the dining rooms, which had an original fireplace from when the inn was built, and I started to lose my equilibrium.

A lady was standing in the room, wearing colonial-era clothes. She told me that I was mistaken. This wasn't a dining room, it was the kitchen. I attempted to converse with her but didn't get any meaningful response.

I couldn't concentrate properly due to getting increasingly dizzy to the point of illness. I had to leave that room and the colonial lady. Once I got into the next room, my balance returned and I felt much better.

That next room was a bar. I saw an older man sitting at the bar nursing a drink. I got the distinct impression that he was a retired soldier. He seemed to be a nice fellow who was comfortably keeping his own company, needing no companionship.

There was a second man sitting at a table next to the bar, counting money and keeping the books. I couldn't linger because that fellow was smoking a particularly noxious cigar that was making it difficult for me to breath.

We went upstairs, where I saw a lady in eighteenth century clothing pacing the hallway.

I followed her to the end of the hall and indicated a

place in a room there for the team to set up a camera. That room was occupied by another lady from long-gone years. She was sitting at a mirror primping and adjusting her hair and makeup as though getting ready for a date.

The next room I came to was a sitting room occupied by a couple who gave the impression of wealth. The wife was contentedly sipping tea while her husband stood nearby.

Then I walked down the hall and came to a locked door. I asked and received permission to enter what was described to me as simply a storage room. The room was a small one and didn't even have any ventilation.

As soon as I walked in there, I felt a strong presence. Turning around, I spotted a young girl's dress hanging on the back of the door. I was told that the occupants found that dress in the building and hung it on the door. The dress was a simple one of the style that pioneer children wore in the 1700s.

I started asking questions, and the dress started swaying on its hook. When I stopped asking, the dress stopped swaying. I started asking again and the dress started swaying again.

To make sure that I'm actually conversing with someone, I often ask the same question multiple times using different wording. That way, I can compare answers and check for consistency. After I asked for the third time, I no longer got any response. The dress lay limp and unmoving, and the feeling of a presence was lost. So we moved on.

We moved down the hall to a large communal living area, where I felt the presence of a family. It dominated by what I can best describe as a father figure, a patriarch.

While talking with him, I learned that he was the owner of the inn. He said it served as his home as well. He asked me to inform the current owner that he was there and would watch over the place. I passed the message on to the

We Don't Talk About Those Kinds of Things

current owner. He appreciated the information and was pleased that the former owner was looking out for both their interests.

That pretty much finished up the main building of the inn, so we went over to the old barn out back that was being used for storage. In the lower level of the barn was a worker who didn't want anything to do with us. He kept hollering for us to leave. He said he had a lot of work to do and didn't want any interference.

Right then John noticed that his digital voice recorder had stopped working. I checked mine and found that it had stopped working as well. They refused to work again until we left.

Well! It was obvious that we weren't welcome in the lower level of the barn, so we went to the upper, ground level of the building.

As soon as I got there, I had a vision of a car that crashed through the side of the barn and I smelled the acrid smoke. The owner of the inn verified that a car had indeed crashed through the side wall of the barn and had caught fire a few years back. When we left the barn, our digital voice recorders started working again.

Right after that, I stopped receiving anything. The walk-through was over. I was exhausted from all the energy I had expended communicating and trying to communicate. And I still had a long drive home. But I had given John good advice on where he should place his equipment for best results.

On that day, unfortunately, we didn't get much in the way of hard evidence, but I got some validation of the information I had received.

The complete investigation at a later date went pretty much the same way: not much in the way of empirical evidence.

Personally, I blame it on the snake.

Bev LaGorga & Ed Kelemen

She Fell to Her Death ... And Nobody Remembered

Some people may disagree, but I think Facebook is a wonderful thing. It has allowed me to reunite with old friends and keep in touch with new ones. One day I was chatting with my friend April.

We were exchanging the usual inconsequential b.s. that friends do just to keep up to date with the daily happenings in each other's lives when I felt compelled to ask her a question.

With no conscious effort on my part, the words flowed from my fingertips to the keyboard and onto the screen, asking if she was working on a certain case that had been getting some coverage in the media. I can't go into the details of the case or its location because I was sworn to secrecy.

"Yes," she answered. "How do you know about it?"

"April," I answered, "during our conversation, I have been getting lightning flashes of happenings appearing in my consciousness like black-and-white photos."

I described what I was getting, feeling that she needed to know, since the case involved murder. I told her what I picked up on through my visions, and she validated those details she could confirm. She asked me to consult at the walk-through, but the date conflicted with unchangeable plans that I had already made. So I asked her to email me a picture of the house. I would see what readings I could garner from it.

As soon as I looked at the photo, my mind filled with visions crowding one another and jostling to be in the forefront of my consciousness.

I couldn't type fast enough to keep up with them.

Finally I had to stop typing and start jotting my impressions down on paper to form into an email later.

The flood of information didn't stop with the physical presence of the picture. When I went to bed that night, I was assailed by scenarios of intense activity. That house was a vessel of death!

Three things competed for attention in my visions: a killer, a victim, and a little girl who had nothing to do with either of them.

It was the little girl that took over my attention. She was so young, so pretty, and so full of life. She played incessantly with her favorite toy, a ball, taking it with her everywhere.

The scene shifted, shaking me to my very foundation. The little girl fell. There she was, her lifeless body lying at the bottom of a flight of stairs in that damn house.

It wasn't just a vision; I transported across time and space to be there. My eyes filled with tears as I returned to the present.

When I told April about the little girl, she was surprised, but she said she'd see what she could find out. A few days later, she told me that the residents of the house said they had just forgotten about the little girl. They were shocked to hear that April and her team knew about something that had happened there that nobody had told them about. How sad it was for the little one to fall to her death and be forgotten.

April went on to say that the residents had invited her team back to another in-depth investigation. She asked if I would consider being part of that investigation.

As luck would have it, the follow-up investigation was scheduled smack dab in the winter, and I didn't want to drive that far alone, after dark, in the snow. I still have an open invitation to that house. I just hope it's not in the middle of winter.

Bev LaGorga & Ed Kelemen

The Geyer Theater
Scottdale, PA

It seemed destined to be an interesting night. An intense summer storm had just passed over the area, and the streets, sidewalks, and parked cars glistened with rain. The air fairly crackled with leftover electricity from the lightning. As we approached the theater, a rehearsal of *Joseph and His Amazing Technicolor Dreamcoat* was winding up, a sure sign that any otherworldly denizens in the theater would be stirred up.

As if that weren't enough, my investigating partner, Denny, was ill. Instead, I was accompanied by two of my friends, Ed and Brendan Kelemen, a father-and-son team. Ed was completely untrained, although he had conducted numerous interviews with people who have had interactions with the paranormal universe. Brendan had been on a very few paranormal investigations but was not familiar with our techniques.

What the two lacked in experience and expertise, however, they made up with enthusiasm.

As with all investigations, I went in cold. I did my utmost to avoid learning about any previous paranormal investigations or reported occurrences at this century-old theater brimming with historical significance. As I've said before, this is how I avoid having any subconscious influences enter my investigation.

Approaching the theater, we were greeted by a lighted marquee and entrance way reminiscent of the golden age of theater.

We met Brad Geyer, president of the theater, at 9:00 p.m. He gave us a tour of this wonderfully restored example of early 20th-century baroque opulence complete with

We Don't Talk About Those Kinds of Things

damask-draped faux windows and gold-highlighted carvings adorning the ceiling. Brad regaled us with a brief history of the theater and its many incarnations as an opera house, vaudeville venue, movie theater, and high school auditorium, and its reincarnation as a community theater since 1987.

While Brad was showing us around, I saw a black shadow coming from the area of the stairs leading up to the control booth. He passed us by and then turned around as though to give us the once-over.

When he did that, I could see that he was an older gentleman with a thin build. After looking us over, he walked on down the hallway of the second-floor apartment cum theater offices and disappeared. I believe him to be the essence of John C. Bixler, manager and owner of the theater during the 1950s. That second-floor apartment behind the theater's balcony level served as Mr. Bixler's home for many years.

After Brad left the theater in our hands, I asked Ed to set up a digital video camera on the left wing of the balcony facing back to the center of the balcony, including the exterior of the control booth. By that time, I had already commenced digital voice recording. (Ed started his digital recorder at 12:30 a.m.)

I had a vision of a well-dressed gentleman wearing a gold pocket watch calmly smoking in the center balcony section. I hoped to get an image of him on video.

While we were setting up on the balcony, we constantly heard footsteps and conversation that sounded nearby. However, we couldn't make out what was being said. It was a constant background murmur, as though a number of people were talking among themselves. Ed said that it most closely resembled the conversational sounds of an audience between acts and during intermissions in the theater.

After Ed got the camera set up, we took readings with

the K II meter throughout the entire balcony area. We got many readings in the yellow range, which is the third light on a five-light meter.

What an active night at the theater! Within the first hour, I encountered the shadow of a former resident, we all heard footsteps, and we all heard disembodied conversations.

This gave me the idea to set up a trigger item, an object that paranormal entities can interact with to provide evidence of their presence to those of us on this side.

For this night, I decided to make sure that all the seats in the theater were in the up position except for two seats in the down position: the trigger items. If a spirit wanted to make his or her presence known in a physical manner, he or she could either raise one of the seats that were down or lower one of the seats that were up.

While Brendan continued to search the theater with the K II meter in hopes of finding hot spots, I had Ed set up another digital camcorder, this one on the stage facing the audience seating area. While he was doing so, he jumped when hearing the sounds of heavy footsteps on the stage left forward wing, right behind him.

As soon as he recovered from that shock, he found that the memory card in that camera was locked and incapable of recording video. At that point, I informed him that there was a spectral woman standing behind him onstage, so he started taking pictures of that area with his hand-held digital camera.

Shortly thereafter and throughout the rest of our investigation, we observed balls and streaks of light throughout the entire theater: in the stage area, in the main audience area, up in the balcony, and in the apartment.

Brendan and I checked the digital camcorder in the balcony to see if any of them had been captured by it, only to find that the camera was shut off. I hollered down to Ed that the camera in the balcony was dead.

We Don't Talk About Those Kinds of Things

"No way," he said. "It has brand-new batteries."

"Oh yes, way," I replied.

He came up to the balcony to check on it. While there he explained that he had installed new batteries with an estimated recording time of over three hours and then programmed the camera so that it would not stop recording unless someone physically hit the "stop record" button. He checked the camera's settings, made sure that the batteries were good, and turned it back on.

Less than two minutes later, I looked at the camera's screen and saw that it indicated a dead battery. The screen then showed "Good-bye" and the camera shut off.

While Ed was rechecking the camera, I saw another black shadow, this one walking along the first floor aisle between the seats heading to the rear of the theater. Then we saw more lights streaking across the wall in a different area.

Ed decided to play it safe and put fresh, brand-new batteries in the camcorder. He set it up and turned it on. We left the balcony. Ed went down to the stage level to get some pictures. Brendan and I went to the control booth.

The control booth was occupied. I sensed that John Bixler liked it there. He seemed very comfortable, enjoying relaxing in the operator's chair. Sometimes he would stand up and look out the window overlooking the theater. He still considers it "his" theater, and he likes to keep an eye on the place. I started asking questions, and Brendan explained the purposes of the various things in the control booth.

Suddenly I heard what I thought was Brendan asking, "Can you hear me?" I felt confused because I thought I'd missed something he had said, but it wasn't him. It was someone else, although there were only the two of us there at the time. Ed was downstairs, two floors away.

Brendan started speaking again. Just as he spoke, I distinctly heard, "Shhh." Again I thought it was Brendan, shushing me because he had heard something, so I stood there quietly listening. Again, it wasn't Brendan. I didn't hear anything else, but I did sense a presence.

We decided to go down again to John's apartment, but we never made it there because we heard Ed calling for us. Brendan and I went to the balcony railing to talk with Ed. But after standing there for a few moments, I started getting dizzy and disoriented, so I stepped back from the railing. Ed came up to the balcony.

While we were talking, we again heard footsteps that sounded as though they were coming from the apartment, so we went to investigate. While we were in the front room, the one we believe to have been John's living room, I became dizzy, disoriented, and nauseated. I sat down for a few minutes to regain my equilibrium. Ed mentioned that he could feel someone breathing on the back of his neck. It was giving him goosebumps.

Feeling a bit better, I made ready to leave the apartment. Brendan was a step or two back and to the right of me. The streetlights coming through the windows cast my shadow on the wall as we walked, and I thought I could see Brendan's shadow alongside mine. I asked him to move. He leaned his head out to the left and straightened back up again, which satisfied me that the shadow was Brendan's. He told me someone taller than us was standing behind him I looked in that direction but didn't see anyone.

Whatever entity was standing behind Brendan heard me and was actually standing in Brendan's shadow because when the figure's shadow moved his head side to side, Brendan did not. And I could then see two separate shadows on the wall.

After a bit I could no longer feel a presence, so we left the apartment and went to check on the digital camcorder on the balcony. It was off again. So we changed the batteries in it again, as well as in the hand-held camera.

We Don't Talk About Those Kinds of Things

We continued to capture paranormal evidence in John's apartment, the balcony, the first floor, and the green room (actors' dressing room).

The Geyer Theater is a huge facility; it was impossible to cover it all in the four hours we were there.

After continually running back and forth, upstairs and down, checking on camera batteries, and trying to investigate, we were exhausted. We gathered up our gear, made sure the building was secure, and left.

The next day, Ed called and told me the camcorder on the balcony had gone through twelve AAA batteries during the course of our investigation. In one instance, he was actually able to watch the battery charge indicator show the battery draining over a period of less than two minutes. He also said that all twelve batteries were brand new, fresh out of the box that night.

As if that weren't strange enough, he checked the batteries the next morning, and all twelve batteries showed a full charge again. He also mentioned that he was able to unlock the memory card in the other camcorder only after leaving the theater.

Over the next few days, Denny and I went over all the video and audio recordings that we obtained that night. There was an absolute plethora of EVPs recovered from the recordings.

For example:

- At one point I ask who is present with me. A reply is made via EVP: "James."
- Later on I realize that a number of people are all trying to get my attention, so I ask, "How many people are here?" The answer comes back via EVP, "Eight."
- Sounds of footsteps.

- A whine like a child not getting his or her way.
- Many sighs.
- "No."
- "Yes."
- "Hello?"

This is just a small sampling of the many EVPs that were recorded. It was quite a night. After reviewing the video and audio, we met with Brad Geyer for the reveal. He was able to listen to all the EVPs. He was quite impressed with the evidence we had been able to gather.

Based on what I was able to determine with two untrained assistants and the potential of the theater, I asked for and got permission to conduct an in-depth investigation with Denny, my partner. We will use all the equipment at our disposal: digital recorders, infrared capture camera, geophones, and more.

We Don't Talk About Those Kinds of Things

Phase 8 – What's next?

We Talk

    I have had many disquieting and otherworldly experiences in my life. Though they've been going on since I was a little girl, I still don't truly know what is happening. I've been told that I am a sensitive, an empath, a psychic, and a medium. A medium can talk with spirits and hear their replies. To me, it's just like having a conversation with a live person sitting next to me.
    I wonder what you think. Is it possible for me to be all these things? As I sit here writing this, the only living person in this room, I hear several voices say yes.
    You decide.
    As for me, I'm just looking ahead to whatever tomorrow may bring. I serve as a consultant for a paranormal

investigative team. I have good friends on this team who call me for help whenever they need it.

Many of my friends have told me that I should write a book about my experiences to help other people who find themselves in a situation similar to mine. So I have. I spent a lot of years worrying about my mental health before I accepted my abilities. I just want you to know that if you hear voices or feel strange sensations when no one's there, you're probably not crazy either. Maybe you're psychic.

I've come to feel that this is what I am meant to do with my abilities. I want to help people, to bring them closure and peace of mind. I've taken the first steps on a journey that I believe will last the rest of my life. I can't wait to see where it will take me and what I will learn.

And just in case you were wondering–now we do talk about those kinds of things.

Bev LaGorga & Ed Kelemen

GLOSSARY

Terms Used in This Book

There are many terms that are used in both investigating and experiencing the paranormal. Throughout my story, I have tried to avoid using too many technical terms that the average person would not know. But it occurs to me that you might find them interesting and that knowing them might help you understand the jargon used by psychic investigators, mediums, and others in the profession. So I'm including this glossary.

Baseline Tests
These tests are performed at the beginning of an investigation to determine natural causes of things like cold spots, drafts, EMF readings, and creaky floorboards. When the actual investigation starts, these items can be disregarded since there are natural explanations for them. *See page 108.*

Clairvoyance
Clairvoyance is the ability to see. One form of clairvoyance, called **precognition,** means seeing into the future. The other, **retrocognition**, is the ability to see into the past.
An example of **precognition** would be when I had a vision of what was going to happen to the woman at the supermarket. **See page 61.**
Retrocognition is what happened when I was transported back in time and observed a man from an earlier time in the office at West Overton. *See page 78.*

Clairsentience/Psychometry

This goes hand in hand with **clairvoyance**. It involves the sense of **touch**. I was transported back in time when I touched Mr. Overholt's desk. *See page 78.*

Clairaudience

Clairaudience involves the sense of **hearing**, as in hearing my name called, conversing with and listening to spirits, and hearing footsteps. *See page 68.*

Claircognizance

This is the sense of **knowing** something without any outside cues. For instance, I just knew beyond a doubt that my grandmother was at my wedding, even though I didn't see or hear her there. *See page 22.*

Digital Video Recorder (DVR)

Digital recordings are based on interface between whatever is being used as a video-capture device and the computer, whether on a hard drive, a DVD, or a flash drive. DVR systems are widely used as surveillance tools and are valuable assets for paranormal investigations. One of their main advantages is that multiple cameras can be set up with minimal supervision of the devices. *See page 70.*

Electromagnetic Field (EMF) Meter

A device that detects fluctuations in magnetic fields, electric fields, radio frequency, and/or microwave energy. I use one of these in all my paranormal investigations because spirits use energy to manifest themselves and that energy usage is detected in changes in the EMF around them. *See page 57.*

Empathy

Empathy means sharing other people's feelings. An **empath** feels others' emotions literally, as strongly as they do. I was able to feel my dad's sadness and regret when he realized that he couldn't do all the things he wanted to with his grandson. And I experienced what that poor murder victim was going through. This is one reason I try to avoid concentrations of people. It's overwhelming to feel all the emotions running loose from everyone. I have to do a lot of blocking in these situations just to maintain stability. *See pages 37 & 66.*

EVP Recorder (also called a Digital Voice Recorder)

EVP stands for electronic voice phenomenon, a voice that appears on a digital recording of a question-and-answer session between the paranormal investigator and a spirit. It is one of the many ways the spirits manifest themselves. Quite often when the investigator asks questions of a spirit, there is no overt audible answer. But if the session is recorded with a digital recorder, both question and answer can often be heard during the playback. For some reason, EVP recorders are more sensitive to the spirits' communications than human ears. *See page 131.*

Geophone

A geophone is a device used to measure ground motion and vibrations. In paranormal investigations it is used to record the physical properties of spectral footsteps, banging, doors slamming, and the like. It is usually placed on the floor of a room to pick up these events.

Infrared (IR) Camera

The infrared spectrum is a longer wavelength of electronic radiation than can be seen by the human eye. Infrared cameras are capable of "seeing" in the infrared range. They use filters or special lights that allow them to record in extremely low-light conditions. We frequently use IR cameras. *See page 131.*

Intelligent Haunting
Simply put, an intelligent haunt is a spirit who is capable of interacting with living people in any of a number of ways, including speaking, touching, and audio recordings. Intelligent haunts can ask and answer questions and make their needs known. A good example is found in my exchange with the older couple in the balcony. *See page 118.*

Intuitive
A term used to describe a person who is psychically sensitive. It is interchangeable with the terms *psychic, sensitive,* and *medium* and is perceived as a more acceptable term among those with the gift. See **Medium, Psychic,** and **Sensitive.**

K II Meter
A device that has five lights in a row that light up sequentially as it detects an electromagnetic field or energy passing in front of it. Its series of lights makes it easier to read than a digital readout. **See page 57.**

Magnetometer
A device used to measure fluctuations in the ambient magnetic field. K II meters function as magnetometers. **See K II meter.**

Medium
Someone with the ability to commune with the entities existing in the paranormal universe, whether you call those entities spirits, ghosts, or shadows. See **Intuitive, Psychic,** and **Sensitive.**

Mist
A fog-like image that is often captured in a photograph (digital or not) that was not visible when the photo was taken. Often it is the result of condensation on lens.

Motion Detector
Any piece of equipment used to detect motion. A geophone is one example of a motion detector. It is often wired into an alarm to indicate possible spirit interference with inanimate objects or to indicate the unwanted/ unauthorized entrance of humans into an area.

Polarized Lens Filters
The use of this filter on a camera minimizes capturing dust motes that are sometimes mistaken for orbs in a photo.

Portal
A portal is a door, an opening between the universe of humans and that of spirits where the spirits can freely pass between the two planes of existence. *See page 108.*

Psychic
A person who has the ability to see, hear, feel, and/or perceive information beyond the five human senses. Because of negative connotations associated with this title, many people with this ability prefer not to be called psychics. People having this ability are also said to possess a "sixth sense." See also **Intuitive** and **Medium.**

Residual Haunting
An empty reflection or imprint of a past occurrence, it is a psychic recording of something that happened. You can observe it, but you cannot interact with it. *See page 52.*

Reveal
   The reveal comes after the investigation is completed, when the paranormal team *reveals* its findings to the client. *See page 109.*

Sensitive
   The term many people with psychic abilities prefer to use to describe themselves. It means psychically sensitive. See also **Intuitive, Medium,** and **Psychic.**

Shadow People
   This is a particular kind of spirit manifestation wherein witnesses catch just a glimpse of movement on their peripheral vision. It is usually a brief encounter, although there are reports of longer sightings. There is speculation that shadow people are not human, but that is unproven. *See page 126.*

Telepathy
   Knowing what is going on in someone else's mind, commonly called mind reading. Being able to finish people's sentences for them is one form of it. Another is knowing what someone is going to say before he or she says it. *See page 58.*

Trigger Objects
   Objects used to indicate the presence and activity of spirits. For example, a kickball may be placed on a bed, its position and location documented. It is then checked later to see if it has been disturbed. Among the many other items used as trigger objects are talc, wind chimes, and pendulums. *See page 127.*

Vortex (plural **Vortices**)
   A vortex is another word for a portal. See **Portal.**

About the Authors

Beverly LaGorga currently lives in a quiet, unhaunted little home in a small western Pennsylvania town with the two loves of her life—her husband John and her son Jeremy. She and Dennis Overly, founded the Westmoreland Paranormal Research Team of Pennsylvania. Beverly has a Facebook presence, welcomes friends and can be reached at bevlpsychic@yahoo.com.

Ed Kelemen is a writer, columnist, and playwright who lives in a small west central Pennsylvania town with his wife, two of his five sons, a pair of humongous dogs, and a clutch of attitude-ridden cats. His articles and short stories have appeared in numerous local, regional, and national publications. Visitors are always welcome at his website, www.ekelemen.com, and he is also easily found on Facebook.